The Light Giver
Stories Workbook

ACTIVITIES AND LESSONS FOR SOCIAL EMOTIONAL LEARNING

The Light Giver Stories Workbook

PEGGY D. SIDERATOS

Illustrated by Stamatia Mavrikos

For the Love of Children Press
Brooklyn, New York

Copyright © 2019 by Peggy D. Sideratos

Published by For the Love of Children Press

Brooklyn, New York, 11209

All rights reserved.

This book may not be reproduced in whole or in part without written permission from the publisher, except by a reviewer who may quote brief passages in a review; nor may any part of this book be reproduced, stored in a retrieval system, or transmitted in any form or by any means, electronic, mechanical, photocopying, recording or other, without written permission from the publisher.

The Lightgiver Stories Workbook ISBN: 978-1-7334620-1-3

The Lightgiver ISBN (Hardcover): 978-1-7334620-0-6

The Lightgiver ISBN (Paperback): 978-1-7334620-2-0

Editing by Red Letter Editing, www.redletterediting.com

Cover and interior illustrations by Stamatia Mavrikos

Cover and interior design and layout by Constellation Books Services

Dedication

This book is dedicated in gratitude to God for His inspiration and guidance and to my amazing family. Daddy, I miss you and I hope you realize the incredible impact you made in my life. Mom and Steven, thank you for your unwavering love and support and for helping me to pursue this dream. God blessed me with the most incredible and loving family. My heart overflows with love and admiration for you.

Contents

1. Decisions, Decisions: 5
   What Do You Do When You're Not Sure What to Decide
   (Follow-up lesson to "The Light Giver")

2. The Treasure Chest: A Tool You Can Use to Encourage Yourself   9
   (Follow-up lesson to "Gabriel's Journey")

3. Secret Messenger (Follow-up lesson to "The Messenger")   15

4. How to Handle Criticism and Words That Hurt: *Is It Constructive or*   19
   Destructive Criticism? (Follow-up lesson to "The Most Beautiful Girl
   in the World")

5. The Happiness Board (Follow-up lesson to "It's Your Choice")   25

6. Positive Affirmations   31
   (Follow-up lesson to "The Big, Ugly, Heavy Suitcase")

7. Is It a Sincere Apology? (Follow-up lesson to "The Race")   37

8. Guilt: The Bug That Won't Stop Bugging You   41
   (Follow-up lesson to "The Guilt Bugs")

9. The Secret Box: Dealing with the "What-If Monster"   47
   (Follow-up lesson to "The What-If Monster")

10. Good, Healthy Fear vs. Bad, Unhealthy Fear   51
    (Follow-up lesson to "Do It Afraid")

11. Sometimes Being Honest Is Scary   55
    (Follow-up lesson to "The Truth Behind Their Words")

12. Gifts (Follow-up lesson to "Let Your Light Shine")   59

13. The Most Important Secret   65
    (Follow-up lesson to "Not Like Everybody Else")

14. What Would a Person of Excellence Do?   69
    (Follow-up lesson to "A Person of Excellence")

15. Handling Disappointment: Is Change Possible? 73
    Determining When to Be Proactive and When to Practice Acceptance
    (Follow-up lesson to "Eleni's Disappointment")

16. Envious Thoughts: 79
    Can We Use Them for Good or Should We Lose Them?
    (Follow-up lesson to "Tommy's Bike")

17. Does That Label Define Me? *Is It the Truth or Just a Stereotype?* 83
    (Follow-up lesson to "Tuning In to Your Truth")

18. The Kindness Boomerang (Follow-up lesson to "Penny's Surprise") 89

19. Planning a Trip to a Senior Home 93
    (Follow-up lesson to "A Trip to the Senior Home")

20. Staying Cheerful During the Waiting Game 97
    (Follow-up lesson to "A Double Test of Patience")

21. The Love Week Project (Follow-up lesson to "Love Is a Way to Live") 101

22. There's Always Room for More Love: *Our Ever-Expanding Hearts* 105
    (Follow-up lesson to "There's Always Room for More")

Introduction

Thank you for purchasing *The Light Giver Stories Workbook*. This book of activities and lessons are an extension to my series of stories found in *The Light Giver and Other Stories to Raise Emotionally Healthy Children*. I wanted to create a simple, fun, and interesting tool for parents and teachers to use to support their efforts in raising emotionally healthy children.

We live in a world today with alarming suicide rates and where kids and teens are suffering with greater anxiety, depression, bullying, cutting, and eating disorders. The level of brokenness has continued to escalate, leaving parents and educators feeling overwhelmed and frightened. The children are hurting, and we all need to take some initiative to address these issues. To help, many schools are currently implementing Social Emotional Learning (SEL) into their curriculum. SEL instruction teaches children how to regulate emotions, improve communication skills, foster empathy, build confidence, and make better decisions.

During my more than fourteen years of teaching, I quickly realized the benefits social emotional learning had on my students. I noticed that when kids had more self-confidence and felt better about their place in the world, their academic performance was better, the relationships with themselves and others was healthier, and most importantly, an inner contentment shone through. Recent studies conducted on the effects of SEL instruction on children substantiate my experience. Studies have shown that children exposed to SEL show a significant improvement in their behavior, better control of their emotional skills, and an improvement in their self-confidence. Furthermore, there are significant benefits in students' academic performance and long-term benefits that follow children into adulthood.

As a teacher, I regularly addressed issues of self-esteem and tried to reinforce the tenets of good character through a variety of lessons, but this was quite challenging, as materials were not always readily available for me to use. Like many other teachers and parents already inundated with pressures of meeting children's other needs, I didn't always have the time or energy to invest in tracking down these materials. I decided to create a collection of stories and lessons to address a variety of social emotional topics for children that would be easy enough for anyone to use and wouldn't require a huge investment of time, and that is where the *"Light Giver Stories Series"* came about.

My book, *The Light Giver and Other Stories to Help Raise Emotionally Healthy Children*, is a collection of twenty-two children's stories that address a multitude of social and emotional skills through storytelling and shared experiences. But I didn't stop there. I knew that additional follow-up lessons and activities were needed to address these topics in more depth, and thus this workbook was created.

The workbook contains easy-to-follow lessons, fun activities, and suggestions for discussions to further enhance this learning. The topics addressed are a mirror to the ones addressed in the *Light Giver* stories. Some of the topics addressed in the lessons include learning how to cope with fear, criticism, disappointment, guilt, envy, and stereotypes. Others help children recognize the gifts that lie within them and encourage them to strive to be their personal best without expecting perfection or comparing themselves to others. Still others focus on the tenets of good character, such as kindness, respect, patience, honesty, and integrity, and demonstrate how these traits affect the individual and others.

The Light Giver and Other Stories to Help Raise Emotionally Healthy Children is available for sale from a variety of vendors and through my website, https://www.thelightgiverstories.com/. If you have not yet purchased the book, there is no need to worry, as these lessons can be utilized without having read the stories beforehand.

I have designed this workbook to be as simple as possible to use. A few lessons require some minimal preparation ahead of time, so please read through each one first before sharing it with your children or students in case you need to have a few materials on hand. The majority of the lessons, however, do not require much preparation at all. The text on most lessons can be read verbatim, and all directions included are printed in italics.

While these lessons, activities, and discussions take only a few minutes of your time, I believe the benefit and insights it will provide your children or students are immeasurable. It is my sincere hope that this program will cultivate and nurture children's self-confidence, help them to feel better about their place in the world, and strengthen the bonds between them and the adults who love them.

1
Decisions, Decisions

What Do You Do When You're Not Sure What to Decide

(Follow-up lesson to "The Light Giver")

Sometimes we are faced with decisions that are easy for us to make: "Do you want mustard or ketchup on your hot dog?" "Do you want a glass of water or iced tea?" "Are you going to watch this movie or another?" But sometimes we need to make decisions that are more challenging and require more thought.

When you are an adult, you may face many more of these types of questions than you will as a child. For example, "Which job should I take?" or "Which home or car should I buy?" But even as children, we are faced with some big decisions. "What afterschool clubs or teams do I want to join?" or "Which middle school should I go to?" "I only have two tickets to the show; which friend should I invite?" or "Is this person or friend somebody I can trust with a secret?" When we are faced with tough decisions like these, it's only normal that we feel an enormous amount of pressure. The anxiety and fear of making a mistake can paralyze us from moving forward. The important thing is to remember one key thing: *don't let your fear make the choice.*

Sometimes fear can be healthy. For example, if we are standing in an intersection and see a car coming toward us, our fear instinct warns us to get out of the way of danger. But there is another type of fear, the unhealthy kind, that may prevent us from moving forward. Sometime people become paralyzed about making a mistake or the wrong choice, and they allow fear to keep them stuck.

One of the best pieces of advice I ever heard was, "If you're not sure what to do, don't do anything at all." Now, that doesn't mean that we should never make decisions, it just means that we shouldn't rush to make them if we feel unsure.

Initially, I like to compare my choices to see if there is a clear right or wrong answer. For example, if you found a wallet in the street with a lot of money in it, you might ask yourself, "What is the right thing to do? What is the wrong thing?" Of course, you know the answer: you should try to find out who it belongs to and return it to them, even though a part of you might be tempted to keep it. You know that returning it is the right thing to do, and in the end, you will be proud of yourself for being honest. But sometimes we need to make decisions that do not have a clear right or wrong answer. It is at those times when I like to rely on my *Inner Guidance Voice*.

I always consult my Inner Guidance Voice when I need to make a big decision and I'm not sure what to do. What is the Inner Guidance Voice, you ask? It's a quiet, little voice inside of you that always knows what's best for you. It's like having your very own navigation system. This voice is always a positive one. It will never say anything hurtful or mean, and when you hear it, you will feel a peaceful feeling inside. That's how you know it's not your fear talking. The Voice of Fear will try to scare you, while the Inner Guidance Voice will make you feel at ease and peaceful.

The following paragraphs with asterisks (*) include references to me and my life. Please feel free to customize the content to reflect examples of your own life, or use the ones here and refer to them as a friend's experience.

*My Inner Guidance Voice has helped me to make some quite important decisions in my life. It once guided me to change jobs, it helped me reach out to a person who became a good and trusted friend, and it helped me decide which college to go to, as well as many other things over the course of my lifetime.

*While I always try to listen to my Inner Guidance Voice, there have been a few times when I couldn't hear it. I think it's because I was so nervous and fearful that I didn't allow my mind to get quiet enough to hear it—but then I learned a trick to help me hear it once again.

When you have been trying to hear from your Inner Guidance Voice but are not having any luck, the best way to hear it again is to begin helping people. Now, I know this may sound like a strange way to "open your ears" again, but it works. Start being especially nice to others. You could help someone with chores, show a loved one how much you love and appreciate them, or offer an ear to somebody who needs to talk about something that's bothering them. You will be amazed by how serving others will help you hear from your Inner Guidance Voice again.

This method works because it is the best way to block out the fear that sometimes gets in the way. Picture fear as a big bully that is trying to block your Inner Guidance Voice. When you start doing kind and loving things, you block out that fear and begin to feel wonderful inside. The joy you feel makes the fear shrink in size and lose its power. The more wonderful things you do, the more it shrinks, and the less it blocks the Inner Guidance Voice.

Activity

For this activity, you will be demonstrating that the more attention we give to fear, the more it grows, and the less able you are to hear from your Inner Guidance Voice.

Materials: You will need a balloon, a dark-colored marker, and an empty paper towel or toilet paper roll. Prior to starting the activity, blow up the balloon, but do not tie it closed. Use the marker to write the word "fear" on the balloon as large as possible, then let the air out again. Write the words "Inner Guidance Voice" on the paper towel or toilet paper roll.

Directions:

Step 1: Show the children the deflated balloon and explain that you will use the balloon to demonstrate how fear works. Begin to inflate the balloon in stages. Each time you blow more air into the balloon, they will visually see the word "fear" grow in size.

Step 2: Explain that the paper tube will demonstrate the way the "Inner Guidance Voice" sends messages. Have the child hold the roll up to their ear, then loudly whisper a phrase of your choice through the tube. (For example, "You are stronger, smarter, braver than you know.")

Step 3: While the child still has the tube to their ear, place the slightly inflated balloon in front of the other end of the tube, obscuring the opening, and whisper the phrase again. Ask the child if the presence of the balloon affected the way they heard the message. Do this several times, inflating the balloon more and more each time, and asking them if it changed what they heard.

Step 4: Explain that when we focus on helping others, our fear begins to shrink, and we are able to hear the Inner Guidance Voice once again. Allow the balloon to deflate completely, and whisper your special phrase again. Ask the child if they could hear clearly now that fear wasn't getting in the way.

Just remember, if ever you are faced with a decision and are not sure what to do, always do what you know in your heart to be the right thing, and listen for your Inner Guidance Voice. When you are making the right decision, you will feel a sense of peace inside.

If you ever have a problem hearing from your Inner Guidance Voice, start doing kind and loving things. Before you know it, the fear will disappear, and your Inner Guidance Voice will come through with the answers you need.

2
The Treasure Chest

A Tool You Can Use to Encourage Yourself

(Follow-up lesson to "Gabriel's Journey")

Everyone faces moments of discouragement and disappointment; it's inevitable, especially when learning something new. I remember when I was first learning to ride a two-wheel bike without training wheels and kept falling down. There were lots of moments when I wondered if I should keep trying or give up. Have you ever felt frustrated or discouraged about a situation? Would you like to share about it?

While it's only natural to experience these feelings, rather than giving our attention to negative thoughts, we need to find a way to encourage ourselves. That's when using a tool like the *Treasure Chest* can come in handy.

Have you ever heard of a treasure chest? If you don't know what it is, allow me to explain. A treasure chest is a large trunk filled with treasures such as gold, silver, and jewels. Would you like to have your own trunk with treasure inside? Well, today you're going to be able to create your own treasure chest, but inside this treasure chest you will not find silver or gold, money or expensive jewelry. The gems inside of this treasure chest will be even more valuable. You are probably wondering what is more valuable than those things. The answer is *joy!*

I know some of you are thinking, "How can joy be more valuable than jewels, and how on earth can you put it in a box?" The truth is, joy is one of the most valuable things a person can have, and while material things can give us some temporary happiness, true joy comes when you feel peace and love in your heart. It cannot be bought, no matter how much money you have in your pocket.

Unfortunately, there are still a few grown-ups who haven't learned that lesson yet. Now, while you can't exactly put joy in a box, you can place examples or reminders of things you treasure into a box, and they can be used to bring you joy at moments when you need it most. Everybody needs to be cheered up at times; even people who are usually happy sometimes feel sad or low and need help to improve their mood. It's at those times when a Treasure Chest may be just the tool to work some magic and bring back joy to their heart.

What kind of treasures are inside the Treasure Chest? The answers are different for each person, because each of us stores our own treasured messages in our own chest. These messages include notes you have written detailing things you like about yourself, inspirational quotes, sweet compliments people have given you, or notes reminding you of accomplishments you have achieved. In a short while, we're going to begin creating this box together, step by step.

Activity

In this activity, the children will be making a Treasure Chest to keep special messages in.

Materials: Each child will need a simple box such as a shoebox, a choice of colored paper, wrapping paper, fabric, and paints to decorate the exterior of the box, and glue to put on embellishments. Each child will need either some strips of paper (at least fifteen) or ten small index cards cut in half to write the messages on, and pencils or pens to record them.

Directions: Have the children decorate their Treasure Chest with the various embellishments. Have them write the messages for the strips that go inside. If necessary, offer to guide them with this. If time constraints are an issue, you can have them continue to work on the exterior of the box independently.

Sometimes children need to be reminded of things they have accomplished or compliments they have received about a job well done. It's important, though, not to force them to include something in their box that they don't wish to put in. This is a tool to shift their mood, and anything that would cause them discomfort is counterintuitive.

While the contents of this Treasure Chest are priceless, creating one doesn't require spending a lot of money. You can use a simple shoe box or any other small box you have around the house for the outer shell. You can decorate it any way you like, because its purpose is to make you happy. Use paint, glitter, stickers, markers, scraps of fabric, and wrapping or colored paper if you like, or keep it very simple; the choice is yours. It may take some time to decorate the outside, so first we're going to focus on creating the contents.

Inside, your Treasure Chest will be filled with little notes to yourself, written on either long strips of paper or on small index cards. Once you finish writing the note, you will fold it up and put it in your Treasure Chest.

Let's get started. On the first set of strips, I want you to write sentences that describe what you like about yourself. I will read you a few samples, but you can make up your own.

Sample Description Sentences

- One of the things I like most about myself is _____ (make as many of these as you like).

- I am a good _____ (friend, sister, brother, daughter, son, etc.).

- I am a kind and caring person and always try to help people.

- I treat people with respect.

- I'm funny (or smart, strong, healthy, etc.).

- I have a warm smile (or nice eyes, etc.)

Take a few minutes to write some of your own now. Can you read me a few of them?

On the next set of strips, write down things about yourself that you are proud of. You may be proud of yourself for doing something that took a long time to learn and master, or you may be proud of yourself for helping somebody else. Here are a few examples.

Sample Pride Sentences

- I worked very hard on my project or book report and did a great job.
- I learned how to tie my own shoelaces (or play a song on the piano, ride a bike, etc.).
- I helped make dinner (or set the table, helped my sister with her homework, etc.).

Would you like to share with me something you have accomplished and are very proud of?

The third set of strips can be filled with wonderful words that others have said about you. You can write them down yourself or even ask the person who gave you the compliment to write it down and put it in your Treasure Chest.

Sample Compliment Sentences

- A teacher said to you, "You write beautiful stories!"
- Your friend told you, "You always know how to cheer me up when I'm sad."
- Your parents say, "We're so proud of you, and love you so much."

A fun activity to do at your next family gathering is to have everyone fill out a Treasure Chest strip for each member of the family and then share them. Once all of them have been shared, everyone can put their strips into their own Treasure Chest.

Can you recall a compliment or words of praise that someone has given you? Would you like to share one with me now? Don't worry if you can't remember any at this moment; once you do remember, you will be able to add it to your Treasure Chest.

I also enjoy including inspirational messages, favorite quotes, or song lyrics that bring me joy in my Treasure Chest. These can also be added.

Sample Quotes and Other Messages

- You are braver than you know.

- After every storm comes a rainbow. Tomorrow will be a better day.

- Today I will choose joy.

- Gray skies are going to clear up; put on a happy face.

- Nothing is impossible if you believe.

If you can think of any right now, record them and put them in. Would you like to share one with me?

When you are feeling blue and need some cheering up, all you need to do is choose a few of your treasures from inside to read, and your spirits will be lifted. You will be amazed at how much better you will feel when you begin to look through your treasures. Just remember, you must keep putting the messages back after you have read them, and continue adding new ones over time.

If you notice a friend or loved one who could use some encouragement or support, write them a little note to put into their Treasure Chest. It will lift their spirits when you give it to them and every time they read it over in the future.

Now that we have many of our treasures ready for the inside, let's begin decorating the outside.

Remember, you can continue to update your Treasure Chest as often as you like. The more time you invest in creating your Treasure Chest, the better and more effective it will be. Have fun making it so that when you see your Treasure Chest and open it, the wonderful energy and joy you felt during that process will instantly make you feel happier.

3
Secret Messenger

(Follow-up lesson to "The Messenger")

Everyone faces moments when they feel sad and blue. You can feel discouraged when you worked on a project and didn't get the result you wanted, or the grade you received on a test wasn't as good as you would have liked, or perhaps one of your friends suddenly moved away. There are many different things that depress us or cause us to worry.

Sometimes, when I begin to feel this way, I try to change my mood by digging through my Treasure Chest. It helps me shift and replace my sad feelings with wonderful ones. Remember, in there we keep notes of things we like about ourselves, accomplishments we have achieved, records of nice things others have said about us, and inspirational quotes.

Sometimes our sad moods can be improved by getting a few words of support or encouragement from a loved one. Another way we can help improve our mood is by helping someone else. You would be surprised at how much helping another person feel better improves your own mood, especially if you do it in a fun and exciting way. Are you ready to take on a top secret job?

Today I'm going to talk to you about becoming a *Secret Messenger*. You may be wondering what a Secret Messenger is and what do they do. As a Secret Messenger, your job is to anonymously write a message to a friend, a loved one, or even an acquaintance in order to either encourage, comfort, or inspire them. (In case you are wondering what the word *anonymously* means, it means that you will not write your name on the note. It's a secret!)

You will write a small note on a piece of paper, fold it if you wish, and place it somewhere they are sure to find it. On the note, you may want to write something describing how special they are, or how much you appreciate something they've done for you or others. Perhaps you could write something to encourage them to stay optimistic through a difficult situation they are facing. When a person gets a note like this, especially when they least expect it, it has such a positive effect on their mood. It can change how they feel about a situation or themselves, and subsequently, it will affect your mood in a positive manner, as well.

A good Secret Messenger looks for opportunities to encourage and help others. Here's an example of a situation where a Secret Messenger can make a difference: Let's pretend that a young boy has just moved to a new city, where he doesn't have any friends. He starts attending a new school and is feeling nervous in his new surroundings. Imagine how he would feel if, on his second day of school, he found a note on his desk that said, "Don't worry, everything is going to turn out just fine." Think about how that note might encourage him. It would let him know that somebody cared about him, and it would give him hope that things will indeed turn out just fine.

You might have a relative or friend who helped you with something you were struggling to learn. Aside from thanking them in person, what if you could give them a secret message saying, "Your kindness to others makes the world a better place." Just think of how that might make them feel.

Your notes don't have to be long or complicated, and you don't need to use fancy stationery or write in fancy calligraphy writing to be an effective Secret Messenger; you can even use a simple Post-It note. What matters most is what is written and the love or support that note conveys.

Is there a teacher, a coach, crossing guard, or a school aid who is especially nice to you? Write them a note telling them, "Your smile makes my day special."

Look around for people who need cheering up, or those who seem worried or anxious, and write them a note. But don't just stop there. Look for people who are especially nice to others, and send them a secret message, as well. You will be amazed at the powerful and positive effect that little note can have on them, and how wonderful it will make you feel, too.

Although we may wish to remain anonymous because it is more fun to leave people wondering about the mysterious sender, there is a chance that people will figure out who sent the message to them. Don't worry if this happens; just kindly ask them to not tell others, in case you want to send a few more secret messages. Explain to them that you are more concerned about bringing happiness to others than getting any attention for yourself. Hopefully, they will respect your wishes. But whether they do or not, don't give up on your mission. Not only will your efforts make you feel better than ever, but you may be surprised to suddenly see new secret messengers springing up around you as others decide to join in on the fun. Who knows, maybe you'll end up getting a few secret messages yourself.

4
How to Handle Criticism and Words That Hurt

Is It Constructive or Destructive Criticism?
(Follow-up lesson to "The Most Beautiful Girl in the World")

"WORDS ARE POWERFUL"

The following paragraph (*) makes a reference to being teased as a child and an adage I was told. Please feel free to substitute a personal story to tell the children.

*As a young child, I was teased by others. My loved ones shared with me the popular saying, "Sticks and stones may break my bones, but names will never hurt me." Well, I soon found out that this statement is wrong. Sometimes words can hurt and can do even more damage than a punch. You just don't see those bruises and boo-boos on the outside; instead, the pain and bleeding is on the inside. What can we do when somebody criticizes us or uses words that hurt us? While I wish I could give everyone a magic wand to make all the painful words go away, I don't have one. However, there are some strategies you can use to help deal with the criticism and handle the pain better.

Step 1: Breathe

The first thing you should do is to stop everything and take five slow, deep breaths. It may not take all your pain away, but it helps your body to calm down and your brain to think better. When you are upset, your body may feel terrible inside, and if this feeling lasts for a while, your body won't work at its best. People who are upset don't always make the smartest decisions, and may have a hard time finding the right words to express how they feel.

By taking five slow, deep breaths, you will instantly calm your mind and your body. Let's try taking a few deep breaths together right now. Breathe in through your nose, and slowly let it out of your mouth. When you breathe in, your tummy should fill up like a balloon. Remember to always do this nice and slow. You will instantly feel your whole body relax. *After taking the breaths together, ask the children if it helped relax them.*

Step 2: Think it over and decide whether this criticism is constructive or destructive.

We need to stop and ask ourselves: Are these words helpful? Can I learn something from them or improve myself in some way? Sometimes a person offers you a piece of criticism to teach you something. This is called *constructive criticism*. When we construct something, we build it. *Constructive* criticism is meant to build you up or teach you something about your behavior.

Here's an example of constructive criticism: Your dad walks into the living room and begins complaining to you about leaving your sneakers out in the middle of the floor again because he almost tripped. "You're always leaving your sneakers out here. Why do I have to tell you this all the time? You aren't being considerate of other people."

When you reflect on, or think about, these words, you may say to yourself, "I'm not trying to be inconsiderate, but I guess if my sneakers can cause someone to trip, that is inconsiderate." This is an example of constructive criticism because it's teaching you something and trying to help you improve yourself while also trying to prevent others from being hurt.

The opposite of this is *destructive criticism*. Destructive words cause hurt and do not offer you anything valuable. It's called *destructive* criticism because when you destroy something, you break it down or pull it apart. It is important to let go of this type of criticism because it is of no value or use to you at all. There is nothing for you to learn from destructive criticism; it only causes you emotional pain.

Here's an example of destructive criticism: While at school, a little girl gets teased about her height by a classmate. "You're so short, you need a ladder to climb over an ant!" The classmate's comments in this instance aren't constructive or meaningful and won't help the little girl learn anything valuable. This is an example of somebody being mean and destructive.

If the little girl chooses to believe this lie and internalizes these words, it will only cause her pain. All she will do is feel worse about her height. Since there is nothing worthwhile to be learned from this comment, she needs to make the decision to let it go. Holding on to destructive criticism is like holding on to poison. The longer you hold on to it, the more damage it can do, and the worse you will feel. The little girl may not be able to stop the boy from saying something mean to her, but she is in complete control of whether or not she allows his destructive criticism to affect her. The wisest thing to do is recognize that it is useless and let it go.

Activity

This activity teaches the children the difference between constructive and destructive criticism.

> **Materials:** To prepare, create a chart like the one seen in chart 1 using a large sheet of chart paper, a poster board, or a large dry-erase board and an appropriate marker. Teachers, you could also use sentence strips and a pocket chart.
>
> **Directions:** Read the sentences below with the children. Discuss whether each one is constructive or destructive criticism, and why. Then place the sentences on the appropriate side of the chart. If you are doing this activity at home, you can make an enlarged photocopy of the chart and either write the sentences in or cut out copies of the sentences and glue them onto the chart.

Chart 1. Constructive vs. Destructive Criticism

CONSTRUCTIVE CRITICISM	DESTRUCTIVE CRITICISM

Let's do an activity to practice differentiating between constructive criticism and destructive criticism. I am going to read you some sentences, and you are going to help me decide in which column it belongs. If it is an example of constructive criticism, we're going to put that sentence under this picture of a construction worker's hard hat, because constructive comments can help build our character and make us better. If we think it is an example of destructive criticism, we'll place the sentence under the garbage can, because this type of criticism is like poison and belongs in the trash.

Sentence Strip Samples

- ❖ Your teacher read a story you wrote and told you the first paragraph was weak and needed to capture the reader's attention better.

- ❖ A kid on the school bus makes fun of your new schoolbag.

- ❖ You borrow your brother's video game without asking and ruin it. He yells at you and calls you careless.

- ❖ Your mom says you are being lazy because you don't do any of your weekly chores and instead choose to watch TV or play video games.

- One of your classmates calls you dumb because you got an answer wrong.
- You tell somebody that you love the song on the radio, and they make fun of you for liking it.

Sometimes it's easier for us to differentiate between constructive criticism and destructive when it doesn't directly involve us, because our feelings aren't affected. It can also be a little more challenging to let go of destructive comments and put them in the trash when our feelings are hurt. If you aren't sure whether a comment is constructive or destructive, you can always ask a trusted friend or relative to help you decide. If it is destructive and you are finding it a little difficult to let it go, remember, as we mentioned earlier, to first take a few deep breaths to help relax your body and mind.

Next, I'm going to share with you some advice I was once told that could prove helpful. A loved one once sat me down and said to me, "Not everything that comes out of people's mouths is true. People make mistakes and many times say things they don't mean. If someone told you that the sky was green with black polka-dots, would you believe them? Of course not—you would know that they were wrong and wouldn't accept their statement as truth. You may not be able to control what someone says, but you are in complete control of what you believe."

I've heard of people who choose to handle destructive criticism in a different way. They write it on a piece of paper, declare out loud, "It's time to let you go," and then rip the paper—and the comment—to shreds. Whatever the method, the important thing to remember is to let it go. If someone had left their jacket behind at your house, you wouldn't keep it, because it wasn't yours. The same is true with someone's hurtful words. They aren't yours, so you do not have to hold on to them. Dump the destructive words in the trash and purposely shift your mind to something that makes you happy.

You might want to listen to some of your favorite music, play a game, watch a funny show or movie, talk to somebody you love, or use your Treasure Chest to make you feel joyful again. And if that thought ever tries to creep back into your mind, and it might, tell it to "get lost," and replace it with a happy thought instead.

5
The Happiness Board

(Follow-up lesson to "It's Your Choice")

Today we are going to begin the lesson with a little thinking exercise. I want you to think about your bed. What does it look like? How does it feel? Think about how comfortable and soft it is when you are lying in it. Think about your fluffy pillow and the color of your sheets. What kind of blanket or comforter do you have on it? Are there any pillows or stuffed animals around it? Picture yourself lying in that bed right now. Nice, isn't it?

OK, now stop thinking about your bed. Don't think about the sheets. Don't think about your covers. Stop thinking about the fluffy pillows or any decorations you have on your bed. Don't think about how nice and cozy it feels to lie in it, especially in the morning.

Now, be honest, are you still thinking about your bed? I know I am, and there's a reason for that. Usually, when we spend time thinking about something and remembering the feelings we have associated with it, it's very hard to stop thinking about it. That's fine when we're thinking about something nice, like our cozy bed. But if it happens to us when we've been thinking about something sad or upsetting, that's not as much fun, and it can be harder to change our sad thoughts and feelings. Our minds can get stuck on an idea or a feeling, and even when we say, "I don't want to think about this anymore," just like the example I gave you about the bed, it still might be on our minds.

Do you know the trick to getting your thoughts and feelings unstuck? The best way to get rid of thoughts and feelings you don't want to hold on to is to replace them with other ones. It's very important to do that if our thoughts are stuck on something upsetting, because if we spend too much time feeling miserable about something, it can sometimes lead to us getting sick.

To help you with this trick, today I am going to teach you how to create a Happiness Board. I bet you're wondering what that is. Well, a Happiness Board is a tool we can use to make us feel better. It is very simple to create one, and relatively inexpensive. You can use a piece of cardboard, a foam board, a cork board, or even a piece of construction paper as your background.

It does not have to be very big; in fact, it can be any size or shape you like. The most important part of this board is what you decide to put on it. On this board you can glue, tape, or pin photos of things that make you happy. You may want to place pictures of members of your family or your best friends on it. You can include photos of places you love to visit and pictures of fun things you like to do. You may decide to include some silly pictures that just make you laugh.

Activity

Have the children make their own Happiness Board.

Materials: You will need foam board, poster board, or a large piece of construction paper. Collect a selection of magazines, downloaded pictures, or copies of photos from a computer. You will also need scissors and glue. (I highly recommend using glue sticks over glue to put things on the board, but if that's not an option, make sure the children use the glue sparingly.)

Directions: Have the children make their own Happiness Board to use when they need inspiration or to raise their spirits when they're feeling sad or bad. They can glue on pictures from the magazines, drawings they made, photos, or whatever else inspires them and makes them happy, including whatever embellishments they choose.

It is helpful for children to see a sample of a Happiness Board to get a visual idea of what one looks like. To inspire them, create a small one on a large piece of computer paper, and glue a few items on the board that bring you joy.

The next paragraph (*) describes what my Happiness Board looks like. Tailor your description to explain what is on yours. If you don't have a sample prepared, simply describe what you would include on your board.

*On my Happiness Board, I placed pictures of my family, my closest friends, my godchildren, and my dog. I also put a few pictures of places I have visited and really loved. I love to go to the beach, so I put a picture of a beach on my board. Some of these are pictures from family vacations, while others are pictures of my favorite places in my neighborhood. I like to include a few pictures of special days and memories that make me smile. Here's one that was taken on a special birthday. Here's a funny picture I found in a magazine that always makes me laugh.

If you don't have a picture of something or someone you want to include, you can always draw your own picture of them, or write their name or the name of the item on your board.

Once your board is ready, it's important to put it someplace where you can see it easily. I keep my Happiness Board in my room, but I don't have it stuck to the wall in case I want to move it. I know sometimes it can be very noisy in one room, so I like being able to move it around to a nice quiet spot.

There is no right or wrong way to use your Happiness Board. You may want to focus your attention on one thing or one person on your board for a few minutes, till you feel better, or you may want to focus on several different things at a time.

Let's practice. Since we don't have our Happiness Board ready right now, we'll do this another way. Close your eyes. I want you to think of somebody who makes you smile. It could be a member of your family, a friend, a teacher, a famous person, or even a pet. Think of that person's face, the color of their eyes, the sound of their voice, and the sound of their laugh. Remember a special moment in time you spent with them. Focus on how happy that makes you feel.

Now take three deep breaths. Are you feeling happier now? By the way, if you are having some difficulty focusing on this person right now, don't worry. It can be more difficult to focus on them when you are not looking at them or their photo. But if you can picture that special person or pet, I want you to pay special attention to any changes you notice in your mood; it can be magical.

Have as much fun as possible making your Happiness Board. You may want to use some magazines to find ideas or pictures you like. Also, make sure if you do use family photos on your board that you don't use the only copy your family owns, especially if you are going to use glue. You can decorate the edges of your board with markers, crayons, stickers, or glitter, and you can change your board whenever, or as much as, you wish. Remember, your board is all about shifting your thoughts and feelings to happy ones, especially on a day that doesn't go exactly the way you wanted. It may not always make the problem disappear, but it can help you feel a little better.

For example, if someone's goldfish died, focusing on their Happiness Board won't take all the pain away, but shifting their thoughts on something or somebody else for a little while might help that person feel a few minutes of happiness that day. If somebody at school said something mean to you, or if you are feeling disappointed because something didn't turn out the way you wanted, use your Happiness Board as a tool to shift you away from your sadness, even for just a little while. When my loved ones are not around or I can't talk to them because they aren't available to come to the phone, just looking at their picture on my Happiness Board helps me feel stronger and happier.

Focusing on unhappy thoughts can make us even sadder. Sometimes we may start feeling sick or begin to believe that things are even worse than they really are. But interrupting those sad thoughts and replacing them with some happy ones helps us forget about our sadness. Not only do our bodies and minds begin to feel better, but they start functioning better. When we feel better, we are hopeful, and usually make better choices about our problems. Being upset all day and night *never* helps anyone.

Right now I'm going to give you a few minutes to start thinking of some things to put on your happiness board. But this assignment is one that requires some time and reflection. You may need some help from an adult to create your board. There is nothing wrong with asking for help to find pictures or to cut or glue some pictures.

Don't put anything on your Happiness Board that won't make you happy, even if somebody else thinks it's a good idea. It must display things that bring *you* joy, and not them. Make sure you leave a few empty spots on it to add things over time. Enjoy the experience of creating and decorating your board, and you will be reminded of that wonderful energy and feeling every time you look at it. I hope your Happiness Board helps you whenever you need it and brings you more peace and pleasure than you ever thought possible.

Teachers, you may choose to introduce the children to the Happiness Board on one day and have them complete it at home, or have them bring in the photos and materials they collected over a few days, and have them work on their boards in the classroom.

6
Positive Affirmations

(Follow-up lesson to "The Big, Ugly, Heavy Suitcase")

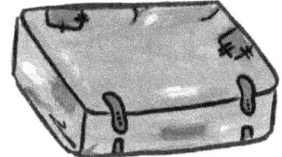

If I came up to you at lunch time with two plates of food—one made from fresh ingredients that smelled delicious, and another that smelled rotten and spoiled, as if it were pulled out of a dumpster—which would you choose? I would bet that the choice would be an easy one to make: you would choose the first plate, with the yummy food. Nobody wants to put anything that looks or smells like garbage into their body. Not only would it taste terrible, but imagine how damaging it would be for your body once it went inside and started spreading through your bloodstream and organs.

Like that toxic food, when you focus on negative thoughts, they can harm your body and make you sick. Science has shown that negative thinking can affect the way your mind works and can eventually cause illness.

On the other hand, focusing on good, positive thoughts is like feeding your body the healthiest of meals, loaded with the best vitamins and minerals. Positive thoughts energize you and make your body and mind thrive and become stronger.

So, if we are to make a choice, much like choosing only the healthiest foods, we should choose to put only healthy, positive thoughts into our minds.

The truth is, this is not always easy because sometimes unhappy, negative thoughts sneak into our heads. When someone does or says something that upsets you, you may start to feel poorly, or sometimes a negative thought can pop into your head all by itself. We cannot control what other people do or say, and we can't control every single thought that enters our minds, but we can push out the bad ones by replacing them with good ones.

One of the best methods I know to do this is by using *positive affirmations*. These are constructive and encouraging statements we say to ourselves that make us feel happier, stronger, and more confident. Most people prefer to recite these affirmations to themselves in private, and not while walking around in a crowd, but there's no rule.

When I recite my positive affirmations, I prefer to stand in front of the mirror, look into my eyes, and say them out loud. I know that might sound a little silly to you if you have never heard of this practice before, but trust me, it's extremely effective. Positive affirmations block out negative thoughts and can strengthen your mind and body by reducing stress, building your confidence, and promoting the use of healthy and helpful thoughts in your mind. I've noticed positive changes in myself since using them; I feel more optimistic and hopeful. To better understand what a positive affirmation is, I'm going to read you a list of a few that I like:

Positive Self-Affirmations

- ❖ I am loved.
- ❖ I am helpful.
- ❖ I am a kind and caring person.
- ❖ I am beautiful.
- ❖ I like myself.
- ❖ I am valuable.
- ❖ I am smart and make good decisions.
- ❖ I learn from my mistakes.
- ❖ I am brave.
- ❖ I have a great imagination and come up with good ideas.
- ❖ I believe in my abilities.

Sometimes people use positive affirmations to help build their confidence. For example, if you moved to new area and had to change schools, you might feel anxious and lonely. Instead of worrying that you might not like your new school or be able to make new friends, you could use positive affirmations to help you. Here are some that might help:

Positive School-Related Affirmations

- I love my new school.
- Everybody in my school in so nice.
- My teachers are wonderful.
- I am friendly and enjoy meeting new people.
- People enjoy spending time with me.
- I make friends very easily.
- I have wonderful friends.

You can use positive affirmations to help you reach a goal you have set for yourself, too. If you want to become an honor roll student, you may want to say a few affirmations to help, along with studying.

Positive Goal-Related Affirmations

- I am smart.
- I work hard and achieve my goals.
- I stay focused on my work.
- I am well prepared for my exams.
- I learn easily and remember what I study.
- I am calm and relaxed when I take tests.
- I am an honor roll student.

You can use your positive affirmations to help you believe the goal you set for yourself is possible, even before you achieve it.

It's important to practice saying your affirmations daily because the power comes from repetition. Sometimes I decide to repeat some of my affirmations over and over because they don't necessarily feel truthful at that moment. For example, if I'm feeling nervous about something one day, I might say, "I am brave and courageous," even if I'm not feeling it at that moment. I keep repeating it, and over time, I begin to feel braver.

Activity

In this activity, the children will discuss various "problem" scenarios and talk about different positive affirmations that would help in each scenario.

Materials: Create a chart like the one shown in chart 2 using a large sheet of chart paper, a poster board, or a dry-erase board. A quick and easy option for home use is to make an enlarged photocopy of the chart and fill in the positive affirmations on the right side.

Directions: Have the children read each sentence in the left column in chart 2 and come up with a positive affirmation that can help the person. Write the affirmation in the column on the right.

Many variations will apply for each scenario. For example, Jason is having difficulty with math. A child might use the affirmation, "I am a great math student," or "I learn math quickly and easily," or "I am smart and can learn anything I want." All of these, and many more variations, are acceptable for each, so long as they align with the topic.

We're going to look at a few examples of issues people might be struggling with and come up with a few positive affirmations that could help their situation.

Chart 2. Positive Affirmations

PROBLEM	HELPFUL POSITIVE AFFIRMATIONS
Jason is having difficulty with math.	
Benny can't tie his shoes.	
Kathy feels insecure about her new haircut.	
Stanley is afraid of the dark.	
Emily is nervous about her skating competition.	

As I mentioned earlier, it is very important that you practice your affirmations often because the more you do, the more effective they become. You don't have to use the same exact affirmations every day. You might want to change them according to your mood or the challenges you are dealing with at the time. Looking in the mirror and saying your affirmations to yourself is by far the most effective way to do this exercise.

However, if you have a trusted friend or family member and you are comfortable trying this, you can do a *Mirroring Exercise* with them. You will need to sit face-to-face across from your friend or loved one and look at each other's eyes when you do this. Person 1 says his or her affirmation, and then Person 2 repeats the affirmation to Person 1, replacing the word "I" with the word "You."

Activity

In this activity, the children will practice saying affirmations out loud with a partner.

Materials: Using chart paper, a poster board, or a dry-erase board, recreate the chart shown in chart 3 before starting the activity.

Directions: Have a child (Person 1) read one affirmation, and then pause so you or another child (Person 2) can read the mirror response to them. Do this for all of the affirmations in chart 3. Once Person 1 has finished their affirmations, change roles so that Person 1 becomes the mirror for Person 2.

Chart 3. Affirmation Mirror Response

PERSON 1	PERSON 2
I am confident.	You are confident.
I am strong.	You are strong.
I can accomplish my goals.	You can accomplish your goals.
I am amazing.	You are amazing.
Let's switch roles now. I will read the affirmations, and you will be my mirror.	

Many people who use positive affirmation have seen wonderful results. Try it out for a period of time yourself, and monitor how it affects your mood and feelings. It is by far one of the best methods I have found to push negative thoughts out of my head, and to help me feel stronger and healthier, both physically and emotionally. I hope it helps bring you a more positive and beautiful future.

7
Is It a Sincere Apology?

(Follow-up lesson to "The Race")

All people make mistakes; it's human nature. We are imperfect and will occasionally mess up. We don't strive to make mistakes or hurt somebody's feelings, but it does happen. When we do make a mistake, though, it is very important for us to recognize it, take responsibility for our actions, and apologize.

Sometimes it's hard to admit that we've made a mistake, and saying "I'm sorry" can be uncomfortable. You may worry that the person receiving the apology will think poorly of you for making a mistake, or be mad at you, possibly for an extended period of time. If you borrowed your brother's phone without asking permission and accidentally dropped it and broke the screen, your brother might be very mad at you, but the situation would only be made worse if you didn't apologize. He would become even more upset with you for not taking responsibility for your actions, and you would probably struggle with feelings of guilt.

Many times, we do not want to apologize because we believe that we aren't the only one who made a mistake. Let's pretend that your friend did something to upset you, and as a result, you lost your temper and said something terrible to them. Even though your friend's primary action may have been wrong, you still need to apologize to your friend for losing your temper. You must take responsibility for your part of the argument, regardless of whether your friend says they are sorry for their incorrect action. And when you do apologize, don't try to make excuses or explain away your bad behavior.

Which of these three apologies seems sincere?

- I'm sorry I said that mean thing to you, but what you did made me so mad, and I couldn't help it.
- I'm sorry for what I said, but you were wrong, too.
- I'm sorry I said that mean thing to you. I lost my temper and said something I shouldn't have.

The correct answer is the third one.

Even if somebody else begins an argument or provokes you to do the wrong thing, you should nevertheless apologize. Do the right thing without any excuses. The first two examples try to justify and defend the wrong behavior. The third one shows the person taking responsibility for their mistake.

When you want to apologize to someone, do it face-to-face, if possible. Sometimes circumstances don't allow it, but if you can, this really is the most effective way to do it. Make sure to look that person directly in their eyes; do not look down at your shoes or look away into space. When you look directly into their eyes, they can feel your sincerity. It is a humbling experience that takes great courage, but it also shows great character as well as respect for others.

It is very important to be mindful of not repeating your mistake. You may ask your friend to forgive you for losing your temper during an argument and calling him a bad name, but if you repeatedly lose your temper or call him bad names, he may not be as forgiving in the future. He may feel that you don't sincerely care about his feelings. We need to try and learn from our mistakes so that we don't repeat them.

There will be times when instead of giving an apology, you may be on the receiving end. It is just as important to be gracious and respectful when others apologize to you. Show them the mercy and forgiveness you want somebody to give you when you make a mistake. You can't expect to be forgiven by anybody if you are not able to forgive someone else.

Remember, making a bad choice or doing something wrong doesn't make you a bad person. Ask for forgiveness, and even if a person is not quite ready to forgive you at the time, make sure you forgive yourself. After all, we are all human. Even though we mess up at times, we usually do and say more good things than bad. Never forget to recognize the good in others and the good in yourself.

I am going to leave you with a beautiful quote I once read on my computer. I don't know who wrote it, but I thought it was so powerful that I had to share it. "The first to apologize is the bravest, the first to forgive is the strongest, and the first to forget is the happiest."

8
Guilt: The Bug That Won't Stop Bugging You

(Follow-up lesson to "The Guilt Bugs")

Have you ever made a mistake? I sure have; I've made thousands of them. I don't try to make mistakes, and I don't enjoy making them. Nobody does, but we make them all the time. We can make all kinds of mistakes. Sometimes we might accidentally hurt somebody's feelings by losing our temper and saying or doing something we wish we hadn't. "You're the worst brother in the world!" We may forget something important, like our mom's birthday, or lose something that doesn't belong to us. "Oh no, I can't find the video game I borrowed from my friend!" We might even tell a lie to somebody to avoid getting in trouble, "No, I didn't eat your piece of pie."

Unfortunately, even if they were made by accident, mistakes can make us feel lousy, especially when they hurt somebody. If we are smart, once we realize that we have made a mistake, we will rectify it whenever possible. For example, if we hurt someone's feelings, we should apologize to that person and ask for their forgiveness right away.

When we know we did something wrong but don't try to correct our mistake, we start to get an awful feeling inside. The longer we wait to correct the situation, the worse we tend to feel. Today we're going to be talking about that awful feeling that starts to bother us when we know we have done something wrong. We're going to talk about guilt!

You may ask, "What is guilt, and why do we experience it?" Well, as I mentioned earlier, we begin to experience guilt when we realize we did something wrong. Our conscience, which is the little voice of truth in our head, wants to feel happy and proud of itself. When we do something wrong, we begin to feel uneasy inside. Our conscience will point out the mistake in the hope that we will take the steps to correct it. It will start annoying us and buzz in our head the way a little mosquito does when it's flying around you. Just like the mosquito, even when we try to ignore it, this guilty voice will keep bugging you. You will hear your guilt buzz phrases in your ear, such as, "You really shouldn't lie to others," or "You better apologize for your mistake," or "That wasn't a nice thing to say."

If we don't choose to correct our mistake, our feelings of guilt will intensify and grow. Some people start to feel physically sick from their guilt. Many often say that when they feel guilty, they feel as if they're carrying a heavy weight on their body, but once they do the right thing, they instantly feel lighter and relieved because their conscience is clear. As uncomfortable and annoying as it can be, guilt can sometimes act as a catalyst, pushing us to tell the truth and apologize for bad choices or incorrect behavior.

For example, if a girl borrowed her sister's bike without permission and accidentally crashed it into a garbage can, causing it to get a big dent, she may anticipate that her sister will be very angry with her. She might be so worried about it that she even considers hiding the bike and denying that she even touched it. But if she does, her conscience, the "little voice of truth," will start to gnaw at her and tell her, "That's not the right thing to do; don't try to cover up your mistake and lie about it."

If she does the right thing and tells the truth about what happened, even though her sister will be angry at her and she might be disciplined by her parents, at least she won't have to deal with the awful feelings of guilt, as well. Her conscience will be clear. When your conscience is clear, you instantly start to feel lighter and more peaceful inside, but if you don't clear your conscience and do the right thing, the "guilt bugs" may appear.

I named those awful feelings I experience when I feel guilty about something I've done wrong the *guilt bugs*. My guilt bugs make my stomach feel like it has dropped to the floor. I feel like I'm carrying a crushing, heavy weight inside of me. When my friend feels guilty about something she's done wrong, her guilt bugs give her a terrible headache and sweaty palms. Some people suffer from lack of sleep and toss and turn in bed all night. The longer you avoid taking responsibility for your mistake, the worse you will feel and the longer the guilt bugs will bother you. They will not go away until you tell the truth or apologize to clear your conscience. How do you feel when the guilt bugs visit you?

I have planned an activity for us that I think you will find enjoyable and amusing. This exercise will demonstrate how guilt bugs can make you feel and show you the best way to get rid of them.

Activity

This activity helps children learn about guilt and how to get rid of the feeling of guilt. It requires a minimum of three players. Player 1 is the "Guilty Party" who made a mistake, Player 2 plays the part of the "Guilt Bugs," and Player 3 is "the Exterminator."

Materials: For this activity, you will need to prepare three items ahead of time. First, create your "Guilt Bug Spray." You will need an empty hair spray bottle or other empty spray bottle. Create a label for it that says, "Guilt Bug Spray" Ingredients: Honesty and a Sincere Apology. You may make a photocopy of the one in figure 1 and cut it out to use. Tape it to the spray bottle.

GUILT BUG SPRAY

**Ingredients:
Honesty and a Sincere Apology**

Next, prepare the guilt bugs. You can download a picture or two of a cartoon mosquito, like the one seen in figure 2, and make a few copies. Cut out the pictures of the bugs and tape them to straws or popsicle sticks.

Figure 2. Cartoon Mosquito

Finally, prepare the "I Made a Boo-Boo" cards. Use three index cards and a marker or pen to create them, as seen in figure 3. Another option is to make enlarged photocopies of each and cut them out.

Figure 3. "I Made a Boo-Boo" Cards

I MADE A BOO-BOO	I MADE A BOO-BOO	I MADE A BOO-BOO
I accidentally dropped a glass and told my mom that my baby brother dropped it. Now my tummy hurts.	I got mad at my friend and called her a bad name. Now my head hurts.	I borrowed my mom's necklace without her permission and lost it. Now I feel like I'm carrying a load of heavy weights.

Directions

Step 1: Player 1, "the Guilty Party," chooses one of the "I Made a Boo-Boo" cards and reads the first sentence aloud.

Step 2: Player 2 is the "Guilt Bugs." While holding the guilt bugs in hand, they circle around Player 1 and make a buzzing sound.

Step 3: Player 1 reads the second sentence on the card and act outs the guilty feeling it describes.

Step 4: Say to the children, "The only way to get rid of those awful, guilty feelings and those terrible guilt bugs is to be honest about the mistake you made and apologize." Ask, "What would you do or say to the person who was wronged by this mistake?" Some children may need to be reminded at this time what qualities make for a sincere apology, as per the previous lesson.

Step 5: Once Player 1 has apologized, Player 3, "the Exterminator," reads the label on the empty spray bottle. Player 3 then pretends to spray Player 2, the guilt bugs.

Step 6: Say to the children, "Once the guilt bugs are sprayed, they disappear." Tell Player 2, the guilt bugs, to fly away. The formerly guilty party (Player 1) now breathes a big sigh of relief.

Repeat the steps with each of the remaining "I Made a Boo-Boo" cards. In a classroom setting, you can involve more children by having others play the parts in the second or third round. If you are doing this activity at home, have the three players switch roles for a little more fun.

This exercise is a fun way to demonstrate how terrible guilt can make us feel and also the best way to get rid of the guilt bugs. Remember, guilty feelings surface when your conscience, the little voice of truth in your head, is trying to remind you to do the right thing. Rather than allow guilt to slowly crush your spirit and make you feel sick, do the right thing. Be honest and apologize, and you will be set free from all the pain and the guilt.

9
The Secret Box: Dealing with the "What-If Monster"

(Follow-up lesson to "The What-If Monster")

Activity

*This activity teaches how fear can influence our imagination.
It requires some simple preparations.*

Materials: You will need a shoebox, a pair of scissors, a scarf or eye mask to use as a blindfold, and a large sheet of paper. You will also need a few random objects to place inside the box.

Directions:

Step 1: Cut a hole in the lid of the shoebox large enough to fit a child's hand. You may choose to cover the box and lid with some wrapping paper, aluminum foil, or brown packaging paper to make it more exciting. If you wrap the box and lid, wrap each part separately so you can open and close the lid as needed.

Step 2: Choose three random household or classroom items to use as mystery items. Use items with different textures to make it more fun. In the past, I have used items like a piece of fruit, a large piece of aluminum foil with mayonnaise on it, different types of nuts, a dry sponge, and a thick marker, but use whatever items you prefer and have handy.

Step 3: Secretly place one item at a time in the box. Have the child place their hand inside and guess what is in the box. To make it more interesting, tilt the box slightly so that the item moves around. Record the child's guess (see chart 4), and then open the box to reveal the mystery item. Record what the actual item is.

Step 4: Secretly replace the mystery item with the second and third items, following the same steps as before. Teachers, you may prepare three different boxes ahead of time to move through the activity more quickly.

Chart 4. What's in the Secret Box?

MYSTERY ITEMS	MY GUESS	ACTUAL ITEM
Item #1		
Item #2		
Item #3		

Today we're going to play a fun game called *What's in the Secret Box?* In order to play, you must first be blindfolded. Then, you will slowly and carefully place your hand through the hole in the top of the box and feel the mystery item. There will be no clues given beforehand.

The contents of the box might be something pleasant, or it might be filled with something disgusting. Just think, anything small enough to fit into that box might be in there. Use your imagination to make your best guess as to what it could be. There's no telling what you might find in there . . . or what might find *you* once you place your hands inside. Are you scared or nervous about placing your hand inside? Do you think the mystery item inside might be slimy, sticky or furry? Based on its size, start to think about what might be inside.

Now I am going to ask for a brave volunteer who is willing to risk putting their hand inside to try to figure out what's in the box. I'm going to write your guess on the chart under the column titled "My Guess." Then, we're going to open the box and find out what is actually in there. We'll write down what the mystery item is in the column labeled "Actual Item."

Now, let's compare your guess with the actual item to see how accurate you were.

Once, a young lady who had volunteered to put her hand inside a mystery box suddenly started screaming, "It bit me!" The person who prepared the box started laughing, because the only thing in the box was an apple. The stem of the apple probably scraped up against her fingers when the apple rolled inside the box. Nobody else wanted to put their hands inside that box afterward.

The truth was, this young lady was terrified about putting her hand into the box beforehand. She had allowed her imagination to run wild and was further scared after hearing other people's guesses of what might be in there. Her fear of what might be in the box or of what might happen to her prevented her from figuring out what the mystery item was. She anticipated that the contents of the box would hurt her, and it distorted her feelings and her reaction.

Although this is just a game, the truth is, many of us get nervous and scared when we come face-to-face with the unknown. This is especially true when we face big changes in our lives. When I was a student, I used to get nervous when I had to meet my new teacher in September. I wondered if my teacher was going to be mean and strict or friendly and pleasant. I felt the same way when I started high school and had to make new friends. I kept thinking, "What if I don't like my school and can't find my way around? What if I don't make new friends?" I remember the first time I had to take a major exam. I kept wondering, "What if I don't do well? What if I fail?" All the what-if questions would haunt me.

Have you ever felt nervous about trying something new and unfamiliar? Could you tell me about your experience?

We all go through times when we come face-to-face with what I call the "What-If Monster." Many times, our imagination runs wild and makes us scared about the unknown, just like the young girl who thought the apple in the box bit her. The truth is, some of the things that once caused us to have fear and anxiety often turn out to be among the most wonderful experiences we have. While I was initially nervous about going to high school, once there, I made many lovely friends. Many of the teachers I was once anxious to meet turned out to be wonderful. And I ended up doing just fine on my big exam. What I soon realized was that focusing on the scary what-if questions was a big waste of time.

It's perfectly normal to get attacked by the What-If Monster, even though it may not be a fun experience. What should you do when the What-If Monster attacks your thoughts and tries to take away your joy? I want you to remember the Secret Box activity and the girl with the apple. Instead of being frightened of the unknown, replace those scary what-if questions with positive and hopeful ones. "What if this experience ends up being wonderful? What if I love this new school, home, or job and make some amazing new friends? What if this adventure turns out to be wonderful and exciting?" If you focus on all the wonderful possibilities that can happen instead, you will enjoy your new journey a lot more, and probably end up having more wonderful things come your way as a result.

10
Good, Healthy Fear vs. Bad, Unhealthy Fear

(Follow-up lesson to "Do It Afraid")

Everybody feels fear, no matter what their age, size, or background. It's a normal human emotion. In fact, there is a special part of the brain called the *amygdala* that helps us recognize fear in order to protect ourselves. Some fear is good for us; it helps keep us safe from dangerous situations and attempts to stop us from making poor choices. That's a healthy fear. But there is another type of fear, an unhealthy fear, that can be bad for us. This fear tries to paralyze us and stop us from trying new things. It can steal our peace of mind or try to stop us from following our dreams.

Let's read over some definitions that explain some of the different characteristics of the two types of fear. *(You can write the following definitions on chart paper, a dry-erase or poster board, or make an enlarged photocopy of them. Please review them together in case the children have any questions.)*

Good, Healthy Fear vs. Bad, Unhealthy Fear

Good, healthy fear . . .

- . . . tries to protect us from danger and keep us safe. It warns you not to stand too close to a ledge, or to move out of the way of an object coming toward you that could potentially hurt you.

- . . . reminds us not to repeat past mistakes, like touching a hot stove or running around with a sharp object in our hand, because of experiencing a burn or an injury in the past.

- . . . helps us follow rules that have been put in place to keep us safe and so we don't get into trouble, like stopping at a red traffic light.

- . . . usually lasts for a short period of time, until we are out of danger or are no longer in a situation where it applies.

Bad, unhealthy fear . . .

- . . . can make us feel bad about ourselves. It tries to convince us that we are not good enough, smart enough, or strong enough to do something. Here's a few examples: "Don't raise your hand, because you will probably give a wrong answer," and "Nobody is going to like your speech, and they're going to laugh at you."

- . . . tries to scare us about what may or may not happen in the future with statements like: "You'll always struggle with science; it's a difficult subject area," and "You will never be good enough to be picked for the team."

- . . . may last for a very long period of time, even if we are not in a dangerous situation.

When fear comes your way, you need stop and ask yourself, "Is this a healthy fear to keep me out of danger or trouble, or is it an unhealthy fear?" Healthy fear is usually situational and only lasts for a short moment in time. It might say to us, "Watch out, that box is going to fall on you!" Once the situation is over, so is the fear. On the other hand, unhealthy fear may remain and linger in our minds. Many times, the words *never* and *always* are part of that fearful phrase. Unhealthy fear will point out things like, "You'll never be able to do that," and "You will always be the last person chosen for the team."

Activity

In this activity, the children will practice differentiating between examples of good, healthy fear versus bad, unhealthy fear.

Materials: Use a piece of chart paper, a poster board, or a dry-erase board and an appropriate marker to create the chart shown in chart 5, or make an enlarged photocopy of the chart.

Directions: The children will read through a list of fearful statements and decide whether each one falls under the category of good, healthy fear or bad, unhealthy fear, based on the definitions given earlier. Record their answers on the chart.

Chart 5. Good, Healthy Fear vs. Bad, Unhealthy Fear

GOOD, HEALTHY FEAR	BAD, UNHEALTHY FEAR

Let's do an activity to help us practice differentiating between the two types of fear. After we read a sentence, we will decide if it belongs in the Good, Healthy Fear column or Bad, Unhealthy Fear column.

Fearful Thoughts

- No matter how much you study, you'll never remember all this information and pass this test.
- Don't bother to introduce yourself to those people, they'll probably never like you anyway.
- Don't climb on that ladder; the step is broken, and it doesn't look very steady.
- Don't go to that party with those kids; you know they like to cause a lot of trouble.
- Don't pet that stray dog, he looks like he's sick.
- Duck, that baseball is heading straight for you!
- You'll never be able to ride a bike; you'll keep falling every time you try.

Fearful thoughts are unavoidable. Sometimes, even when we recognize that a fear is unhealthy and not a real danger to us, it can still be upsetting and cause us anxiety. Have you ever been troubled by an unhealthy fear? Would you like to share what your fear was and how you decided to handle it?

As much as we don't like facing fear, we can feel comforted knowing that we are not alone on this journey. All people experience fear, but the important thing to remember is not to let fear make your decisions. You have complete control over how you handle those thoughts. *Brave people feel fear, too; they just decide to push through it and do things afraid.*

Remember, when you are faced with a situation where an unhealthy fear is troubling you, you have a choice to make. *Is what you desire or want to accomplish more important to you than the fear you are facing?* If the answer is yes, then move forward despite being afraid.

11
Sometimes Being Honest Is Scary

(Follow-up lesson to "The Truth Behind Their Words")

Do you get scared sometimes? I sure do. What are you afraid of? I fear bugs, rats, and snakes, and I'm petrified of scary movies. *(Fill in your fears in lieu of mine.)* Everybody experiences some fear, and it's an uncomfortable feeling for us.

There are times, though, when we fear things we cannot see, hear, or touch. Some children, and even some adults, are afraid of the dark, for example. Occasionally, we may be afraid of something that may or may not happen in the future. "What if I don't make the basketball team?" or "What if I can't make it into the school I want to attend?" We might be scared or nervous about upsetting somebody. "How will I tell my little sister that her fish died?" Sometimes it can be scary for us to share our insecurities, flaws, or the mistakes that we've made with other people. We worry that they might think less of us. "Will my friends make fun of me if they find out that I don't know how to ride a bike, tie my shoelaces, or that I still sleep with my favorite teddy bear?" "What if the teacher finds out that I've lost my book?"

Occasionally, we are scared about sharing some of our differences with others because we worry that they won't accept or like us if we have dissimilar ideas or views. Once, my friends and I watched a movie together, and they all loved it. They wouldn't stop talking about how hysterical they thought it was, but honestly, I hated it and thought it was silly. When they asked me what I thought of it, I was very nervous about sharing my true opinion with them. I wondered if they would think I was strange for not liking it. When I did finally tell them, it didn't make a difference to them. True friends will not tease or alienate you for having a difference of opinion.

There are times when we worry about being honest with people because we don't want to hurt their feelings. If a friend of mine was excited about an outfit that she bought and I didn't like it, I wouldn't say, "Boy, that's ugly," because I wouldn't want to upset her. Besides, that would just be my opinion, and others might completely disagree with my judgment. That said, I wouldn't outwardly lie and say that I loved it, either. In cases like these, I try to find something positive to say, such as "Wow, that's a pretty color!" or "That fits you just perfectly," or "I can see how happy you feel in that outfit!" You should always try to be honest, kind, and respectful in a situation like that.

It can be scary when we want to share our feelings with somebody and are unsure how they will react. It may be easy to say "I like you" or "I love you" to people we are already close with, but we might be nervous to say it to a new friend; we may worry that they don't feel the same way. While there is no way of knowing what their response would be, I'm sure that it would be nice for them to hear that somebody cares about them.

We might hesitate to be honest with someone who hurt our feelings. If a person said something mean to us, we might be tempted to be spiteful and reply with a nasty response instead of being honest and saying, "You hurt my feelings." We might let the anger or fear we feel inside of us speak for us instead, and that usually just makes the situation worse. Things would be resolved easier and quicker if we would just tell the truth from the beginning, and not let the argument grow and escalate.

While it can be scary to be honest in certain situations, being honest is the most rewarding and guilt-free way to live. When I start to feel nervous about being honest with someone, I ask myself these three very important questions:

- ❖ Will I be proud of myself for being honest?
- ❖ Am I being true to who I am?
- ❖ Am I telling the truth in a kind and respectful way?

When I can say yes to all three of these questions, that's when I decide not to let fear keep me from sharing my truth.

Activity

In this activity, the children discuss scary and fearful situations and how they might handle them.

Directions: Read over the various scenarios below with the children and discuss how they might decide to handle the hypothetical situation. There may be more than one appropriate response for each one.

We're going to look at a few hypothetical scenarios where being honest might seem scary. After we read each one, we will discuss several ways we can choose to handle the situation.

Scenario 1: You just noticed that one of your classmates is very upset and crying because your best friend was making fun of them during gym class. What could you do?

Scenario 2: Your uncle buys you a sweater for your birthday, and you think it's ugly. What can you say?

Scenario 3: You accidentally deleted your mom's favorite show on the DVR. She mistakenly accused your younger brother of doing it because he was now holding the remote control. What should you do?

Scenario 4: You are invited to a party where many of the kids want to play a very mean practical joke on someone you know. What could you do?

Scenario 5: A friend of yours is very upset because she got a bad haircut and looks terrible. She came over to your house to show you the new cut and asks, "What do you think?" What could you say?

Scenario 6: You just learned that one of the kids on your baseball team was making fun of you because you were playing badly that day. You thought he was your friend. How could you handle this situation?

Being honest isn't always easy, and many times we do experience some fear when we decide to either confess to a wrongdoing, confront somebody for doing something hurtful to another, or want to admit something personal. Generally, once we push through the fear, we experience a great reward. Sometimes the reward is the respect of our friends and family who recognize our courage, integrity, and honesty. Even more importantly, though, is the inner peace we experience in our conscience and the pride we sense inside knowing that we are a good and honorable person.

12
Gifts

(Follow-up lesson to "Let Your Light Shine")

Do you love gifts? Most of us get very excited when we think about gifts, and we usually associate them with birthdays or different holidays when people exchange presents. It's always fun and exciting to rip through the wrapping paper or ruffle through the tissue paper in the gift bags to see what we're receiving.

Today we are going to focus on the kinds of gifts that we all have inside of us. I know some of you may be looking at yourself wondering, "Do you think I'm hiding a video game or a toy somewhere? I'm not carrying any gifts!" But I'm here to tell you that you are full of gifts, and the ones you have are much more valuable and special than any type of present you could buy at a store. In fact, you probably have more gifts inside of you than you could ever imagine. You were born filled with gifts, and they are part of what makes you so special.

What kind of gifts am I talking about? I'm referring to the special talents and abilities we have inside of us. To help you understand this better, I can give you a few examples of gifts some people have, but yours may be completely different.

Everyone comes with a variety of gifts and in different combinations; like our fingerprints, no one has the same exact set.

Some people are gifted athletes and can play sports like basketball, baseball, hockey, and tennis very well. Others are great runners, gymnasts, or swimmers. People can be musically gifted and easily learn to play an instrument, while others have a wonderful singing voice. People can be gifted in the arts and enjoy acting or dancing, while some like to draw, paint, or sculpt.

I know people who are very funny and always make me laugh, and others who are wonderful storytellers. Some people are incredible cooks or bakers; some are wonderful photographers or master video game players.

There are so many different gifts a person can have that it's impossible to list them all. All people have many gifts, and some of you may even have some in common with your friends or family members, but nobody has them all. What kind of gifts do you have? Would you share some of them with me?

Customize the paragraphs with the asterisks (*) to describe your personal gifts with the children, as well as the gifts of another friend or family member. The sample below is one that applies to my life.

*I am not athletically gifted. When I was in elementary school, I was always the last one picked to be on the teams, especially if it entailed running. Whenever we had relay races, I was extremely slow in comparison to the other kids in my class. I didn't enjoy it, either; in fact, running made me miserable. I still don't like to run, even today. As an adult, it doesn't really bother me, but when I was younger, I felt incredibly sad about it. There were many times I would cry, thinking about how poorly I was doing.

I finally realized I could either focus on the things I wasn't good at or focus on the gifts I had. I chose to focus on the things I enjoyed and did well, instead of feeling bad about the things I struggled doing. I realized that I loved to sing and could sing very well, so I joined my school's chorus. Although I wasn't talented enough to become a professional singer, I continued to sing every chance I had because I enjoyed it, and because I learned that my singing brought joy to others. In fact, one of the best parts of having a gift is sharing it with other people and bringing them joy.

*My brother is a marvelous cook who prepares delicious meals. I can prepare a few dishes well, but I'm not nearly as talented a cook, and I don't enjoy it as much as he does. I really enjoy making desserts, though, and I love to get creative and experiment with different types of flavors and ingredients when baking. It makes me happy to see somebody enjoy one of my desserts, and my brother says the same thing about watching someone enjoy the food he prepares. In our home, these two gifts balance out well. He takes care of dinner, and I take care of dessert.

There are other types of gifts you possess that you may not have even considered. You may be a good, trusted friend, an excellent listener, or someone who always knows how to cheer somebody up when they are sad. Perhaps you are a great public speaker. Some people are great at organizing things or putting together pretty outfits. Maybe you are great at doing puzzles or solving mysteries. You may have a talent for math or science, or you may love to create computer programs.

*There are some gifts we possess that we recognize early on in our lives. I knew I loved to sing when I was a little girl, but I didn't realize that I enjoyed making desserts until I was older. I was even older than that when I realized how much I enjoyed spending time with children and teaching them.

Even when we are gifted at something, we still need to work on becoming better at it. For example, if someone is a talented musician, they still need to practice. Athletes still need to train to improve their performance and reach their optimal level.

Activity

This activity helps children recognize their unique gifts.

Materials: Each child will need a small- or medium-sized paper gift bag, a pencil or pen, a magic marker, and either ten to twelve small strips of paper or small index cards.

Directions: The children will write each of their gifts on the strips of paper or small index cards. If they have any difficulty writing their gifts on their own, please record their answers for them. If possible, choose a non-glossy gift bag so the children can write their names on them in marker and decorate them in the future.

> If the only gift bags you have access to are glossy, you may write their names on the gift tag instead.

Think about some of the gifts you possess, then write each one of them on these cards (or paper strips), fold them up, and place them in your very own gift bag. These gift bags are yours to keep. If you realize later that you forgot to write down one of your gifts, or if you discover a new one you were unaware of before, you can always add them.

You may need to prompt some children to recall some of the gifts you know they possess. Whether you are a parent doing this activity at home or a teacher using this activity in your classroom, model the activity by creating your own gift bag. If doing this activity in a classroom setting, remind the students that this is not a competition of who has more. Some children will record many, whether they truly possess the gifts or not. Others might struggle to recognize their gifts for a variety of reasons and may need some extra encouragement.

In a little while we'll each share three (or more) gifts we included in our bags. When we do, you may hear somebody mention a gift that you have but forgot to write down. Don't feel rushed to write it down at that moment. You can always add it later.

As I mentioned earlier, one of the best parts of having a gift is sharing it with others. As we share some of our gifts with one another later, I want you to explain how you might choose to share these gifts with others. If you like, you can record your response on the back of the paper where you have written your gift to remind you to share your gift with others in the future.

(Sharing time)

There is one thing I always want you to remember: nobody in the world has every gift. There is no need to get upset if you do not possess a gift that someone else has. You are not supposed to have every gift. Think of how boring it would be if everyone was gifted at all the same things. Those gifts just wouldn't be as special; they would be ordinary. It's our differences that make us special and interesting.

What if there is something you enjoy doing but you really aren't very gifted in that area? Should you give it up? Absolutely not!

* I may never be an amazing artist, and my work may never hang in a museum, but it doesn't stop me from drawing pictures. Plus, there is always room for improvement, especially if you practice.

Keep your gift bag in an area where you can access it easily, so you can continue to add other gifts you discover about yourself. If you ever feel disappointed because you are not as gifted at something as you would like, look through your gift bag and remind yourself of just how many special gifts you do have. You are unique and special because you are the only person in the whole world with this combination of gifts and with the potential to use all of them to bring joy to others. Never forget that!

13
The Most Important Secret

(Follow-up lesson to "Not Like Everybody Else")

Today I'm going to share with you one of the most important secrets you will ever learn. Despite its magnitude, many people are not aware of it—including many adults. *(The next sentence is optional.)* In fact, I only learned it recently myself; I wish I had known it sooner. After I tell you what it is, you might wonder, "Is that it? It seems so simple." But once you realize its truth and power, and you begin to believe it, it changes the way you look at everything in your life.

The secret is the sentence "I am perfectly made!" Reveal the sentence by visually uncovering it in some manner. Parents at home can whisper it in the child's ear like they are sharing a big secret. Once revealed, ask the children to say the phrase out loud: "I am perfectly made!"

I know you are wondering what this secret means. Does it mean that everyone is perfect in every way? No, that's not what it means at all. There is not one person in this world who is perfect, but we all are perfectly made. To be perfectly made means that you have everything you need to be a perfect you, and that is all you will ever need.

Many times, we make the mistake of complaining about things we don't like about ourselves and wish those things could be different. Our biggest fear is that we are not good enough just the way we are. How many times have you heard someone say, or have you thought to yourself, "I wish I were smarter, taller, shorter, thinner, prettier, more handsome, more athletic, funnier, more confident, more popular, more talented, or better at this or that"? The list can go on forever. Even worse than that, many people start to compare themselves to others. Why can't I be as (fill in the blank) as this person? We focus on the things we don't like about ourselves instead of the hundreds of things that make us wonderful and unique.

We are worried that we are not enough just as we are, but that's a falsehood. The biggest mistake we make is believing that if we could change the things we don't like about ourselves, we would be happy, but that is not true. Loving who you are, and appreciating yourself the way you are, are the only true ways to be happy. The irony is, while we're complaining about ourselves, there is somebody out there wishing they could be more like us in some way.

What we fail to realize is that we are not designed to be just like everybody else. We are created to be unique and special. Nobody else on this planet has the exact combination of your physical traits, your gifts, and your personality. Yet along with these wonderful things, you are meant to have certain weaknesses and faults. It's no accident; it's intentional.

Our gifts and talents are meant to bring beauty into the world, and we love having them. However, as hard as it may be for you to believe, our weaknesses are there to serve several purposes, as well. For one thing, they teach us humility to not think too highly of ourselves. Think of how easy it would be for us to become arrogant and snooty if we were completely perfect. It would have a dramatic effect on our behavior and our beliefs. We would never need anyone's help, and that would be sad, because when we support each other, we bring more joy into each other's lives.

Serving people opens our hearts and makes us feel better inside. It is at those moments when we are our most beautiful. Helping others gives us the opportunity to build relationships with people, especially our family and friends.

Having imperfections also makes us more accepting and sympathetic of others who can't do everything perfectly, either. It short, it teaches us cooperation and compassion.

Could you imagine how utterly boring it would be if everyone were able to do everything well? For example, if we all had perfect singing voices, when one person sang a song brilliantly, it would be no big deal. Our reaction might be, "So what, I can do that, too," instead of, "Wow, what an incredible voice!" When someone has a gift or talent that I don't, I can recognize and appreciate the beauty of it. I wouldn't feel the same way if I, and everyone else, could do the same thing; it would be ordinary.

Each of us has a special purpose to fulfill, great things that we are meant to accomplish. We have all been given the gifts and talents we need to achieve these goals. If you love to paint and draw, you may grow up to be an artist or graphic designer. But if, for example, a person hates talking in front of people so much that they nearly faint every time they stand in front of a crowd, they are probably not meant to be a public speaker. However, that person might be wonderful with numbers and make a great accountant. Your combination of gifts and talents is directly linked to the purpose you are meant to fulfill, and will always lead to your happiness. If you don't have a particular gift or talent, it's because you probably don't need it to complete your purpose.

*The next paragraph is an example that applies to my life.
Customize it to fit your talents, gifts, and weaknesses.*

*I love spending time children; I think they are so much fun. I also enjoy talking to people and listening to them share about their lives. These are gifts I've always had, and they fit perfectly for me to have become a teacher. That's why they were planted in me; I needed them as part of my purpose. However, I am a terrible basketball player. No matter how hard I tried, I was a terrible player and did not enjoy playing the game at all. When I was younger, I use to feel bad about not being able to play well, until someone helped me realize that I didn't need to have that talent to be a perfect me. Now, as an adult, I know that being a wonderful basketball player was not part of the purpose I am here to fulfill, and I feel completely peaceful about it.

Each of us is created with a unique shape, color, and design, much like a puzzle piece. When you look at one puzzle piece, you may not realize its value and importance. It is only when all the pieces come together that you can see the beauty of the whole picture. If one piece was missing, though, it would affect the whole look of the puzzle. Without each piece, the picture is incomplete. It is only when we all come together, sharing our gifts with one another and helping each other with our weaknesses, that the real beauty of this world emerges.

Always remember, when you start to compare yourself to others, or find yourself wishing you were different—*stop*. Instead, remind yourself that *you are perfectly made!* You are a unique and very special part of a perfect plan, even with your imperfections.

14
What Would a Person of Excellence Do?

(Follow-up lesson to "A Person of Excellence")

How many of you appreciate it when someone you love tells you that they are proud of you? I love that feeling, but I also enjoy feeling proud of myself, which is why I always strive to be a "Person of Excellence." You might be wondering what it means to be a Person of Excellence (POE). Well, let me start by clarifying that it does not mean being excellent and perfect at everything. It's absolutely impossible for anyone to be perfect. Rather, a Person of Excellence is someone who shows integrity, is honest and fair, and always tries to do their personal best.

A POE is respectful and demonstrates good manners to everyone, even to people who are disrespectful to them. They always use words such as "please," "thank you," and "excuse me." They show good sportsmanship whether they win or lose a game, and shake hands with their opponent after the game. A POE is trustworthy and always strives to keep a promise. They help people whenever possible, and do not condone or support anyone who tries to hurt others physically or emotionally. They wait their turn patiently, and do not push or shove people on the line or cut in front of anyone. They listen respectfully and do not criticize or condemn people who have different opinions. Lastly, a Person of Excellence always puts their best effort into whatever they are doing, whether it's a job or their schoolwork.

While all of us may strive to be a POE, sometimes we fall short of this goal. We're all flawed human beings who make mistakes and lose our patience. We may lose our temper during an argument and say something that hurts someone's feelings, or tell a small fib. That's why it's important as a POE to learn to apologize and take ownership of our mistakes, even when we're not the only ones who did something wrong. We need to be quick to ask for forgiveness, and be gracious to others when they ask us to forgive them.

Most of the time it's not difficult to be a Person of Excellence, but sometimes it can prove to be more challenging. Here's one example: Let's pretend that you went to a toy store to buy your friend a birthday gift. You want to get them a video game that they really want, but somebody just picked up the last one. You notice that as that shopper is walking away, the game you wanted to buy your friend has fallen out of their shopping cart. What would a POE do? Would they pick it up and run to the register to pay for it before the shopper noticed, or would they go over to the shopper and tell them that something fell from their carriage? *(Wait for a response)*

Even though a Person of Excellence would like to get their friend the gift they wanted, this would not be the proper way to do it. Instead, a POE would pick up the game and give it back to the shopper who accidentally dropped it.

Activity

In this activity, the children are presented with several scenarios and then discuss what they would do as A Person of Excellence.

We're going to play a little game called *What Would a Person of Excellence Do?* I'm going to read a few scenarios to you, and you will respond by telling me how you believe a Person of Excellence would handle each one. *In some circumstances, there may be more than one correct answer.*

Scenario 1: Nancy went to the grocery store, and after she paid, the clerk accidentally gave her too much change back. Should she keep the extra money, which doesn't belong to her, or should she give it back to the cashier? What would a Person of Excellence do?

Scenario 2: Niko and Alexander are playing catch in the street. At one point the ball gets away from them and accidentally breaks their neighbor's car windshield. They look around and realize that nobody else is around to see what happened. What would a Person of Excellence do?

Scenario 3: Bart is invited to his friend Jack's house for dinner. Jack's parents prepared a lovely dinner and the most delicious dessert. After they finish this wonderful meal, Bart notices that the table is full of dirty dishes and glasses. What would a Person of Excellence do?

Scenario 4: Last week, Mary promised to help Missy move into her new home on Saturday afternoon. Saturday morning, another friend asks Mary if she wants to go to a party that is taking place at the same time. What would a Person of Excellence do?

Scenario 5: Ursula borrowed her friend's favorite dress to wear to a wedding. Even though she was very careful while wearing it, at the end of the evening, while waiting for her ride, a truck drove by and splashed some mud on the dress. What would a "Person of Excellence" do?

While being a Person of Excellence isn't always easy, it will earn you the respect and admiration of many people. However, the greatest reward of all is being proud of the person whose reflection you see in the mirror.

15
Handling Disappointment: Is Change Possible?

Determining When to Be Proactive and When to Practice Acceptance

(Follow-up lesson to "Eleni's Disappointment")

*The following paragraph (*) depicts a story about my brother.
You can substitute the story with another or change the existing one
to say, "A friend (or colleague) of mine" instead.*

*My brother *loves* baseball, and he especially loves his hometown team, the New York Mets. He's been a Mets fan all his life, and I think his devotion for them grows with each passing year. It hasn't been easy for him being a Mets fan. They have won the World Series championship only twice in his lifetime, and he was only three years old the first time, so he couldn't enjoy it the way he would now.

In 2015, the Mets made it to the World Series, and my brother had tickets for every home game they played. He was beyond excited, especially since it had come as such a surprise to everyone that they played so well that year—they had surpassed everyone's expectations. However, they lost the Series. It was difficult to watch because they were doing so well at the beginning of the last game. My brother was so disappointed—dare I say, he was devastated—but there was nothing he could do about it. Sometimes we can be proactive and try to improve or fix things, but like this game was for my brother, sometimes things are completely out of our control. There was nothing he could do to change the outcome; he just had to accept it and be a gracious loser.

Disappointment is hard and painful, but it happens to everyone numerous times throughout our lifetimes. Things will not always go the way we want them to. You might try out for the basketball team, a class play, or your school's chorus and not be chosen. Sometimes we lose a game or get a birthday present that we hate. Your favorite television show gets cancelled, or you lose something very valuable.

Adults also face many disappointments in their lives. They don't get the job or promotion they worked hard for, the roof of their house starts to leak and needs expensive repairs, or somebody misses an important meeting because their car broke down. No person on earth can escape disappointment.

When we face a big disappointment, we might want to cry, scream, or get depressed, and sometimes we do. However, it is vital to remind ourselves that the pain and unhappiness will pass, and that the future will bring many other good things our way. The thing is, it's not always easy to believe this when the hurt is fresh.

There are times when we can be proactive after a disappointment. Proactive people still have to accept the disappointment, but they work on making changes that can positively affect the outcome in the future. For example, if you didn't make the basketball team or chorus this year, you have to accept it, but you could decide to practice more and try out again next year. By practicing, you can improve your skills, thus increasing your chances of success in the future. If you don't perform well on a test, while you cannot change your grade on that exam, you can always study harder for the next one to improve your overall average.

Rather than wallow in self-pity and feel bitter about what happened, you can choose to move forward in these circumstances and perhaps change the outcome in the future. However, there are certain situations that don't allow us this opportunity.

If your best friend suddenly moved to another state or country, you won't be able to see them every day. You can call each other and occasionally video chat, but you still won't have many opportunities to spend time together. In this case, you can't change the situation; you need to just accept it. Although you may feel sad for quite a while, and miss your friend terribly, you will now need to get accustomed to living far away from each other.

The key is to realize when there is an opportunity to be proactive and try to make a change and when you have no alternative and must practice acceptance. You need to ask yourself, "Is change possible? Even if I can't change the disappointment I am suffering right now, is there something I can do to alter the outcome in the future, should I choose to?"

Activity

In this activity, the children will learn the difference between disappointment that must be accepted and disappointment that can inspire proactive actions for the future.

Materials: To prepare, make an enlarged photocopy of chart 6, or create a chart like it using a large sheet of chart paper or poster board and a magic marker.

Directions: Read through the list of sentences depicting disappointing circumstances, and have the children decide whether a person could be proactive about the situation or if they would need to just practice acceptance. Write each sentence in the appropriate column.

Chart 6. Proactive Choice vs. Acceptance

PROACTIVE	ACCEPTANCE
There is the potential for me to try again or to change this outcome in the future.	It is not possible for me to change this circumstance.

We're going to review a few scenarios of disappointing circumstances and decide whether you could be proactive in that situation or whether you would need to practice acceptance. If there is the potential to try again or to change the outcome in the future, we will place the scenario in the *Proactive* column. If there is no possible way to change the circumstance in the future, we will place it under the *Acceptance* column.

Scenarios:

- The batch of cookies you baked tastes terrible.
- The concert you wanted to go to is sold out, and you can't find tickets anywhere.
- You wanted a baby sister, but your mom gave birth to a boy.
- The best player on your favorite baseball team got traded.
- You ran for class president and lost.
- Your best friend is grounded and can't come to your birthday party.

❖ You kid brother spilled his juice on your math homework.
❖ You came in second place in the swimming competition.

Would you like to share about a disappointment you have faced? What column would you put it under? How did you decide to handle it then? Would you do anything differently now?

While we may not immediately be able to change certain disappointing outcomes, sometimes being proactive and setting a goal for ourselves assists us in healing a little faster. Attaining these goals also helps us learn to appreciate things differently.

Even when we are proactive, however, we don't always get the results we want. We may try out for the basketball team again and still not make it. Although we cannot always control the way certain situations unfold, we do always have the power to manage our reactions to them. Having a good attitude, even when things don't turn out the way we want them, is the key to moving toward acceptance. Remaining sad or bitter when we are disappointed only steals our joy and peace; it never changes the outcome.

My parents always taught me, "It's how you move forward when you are knocked down that counts." Instead of living in the past and focusing on what you cannot change, begin to look forward and focus on the wonderful experiences and possibilities the future might bring.

16
Envious Thoughts: Can We Use Them for Good or Should We Lose Them?

(Follow-up lesson to "Tommy's Bike")

Every human being feels envious sometimes. We see an object that we wish we could have, or notice a special quality or trait in a person and wish we could have that characteristic, too. You may say to yourself, "I wish I could have a phone like this person's, or a video game system like that person's." Or you may wish you could be as tall, athletic, smart, or popular as somebody else.

*The paragraphs with an asterisk (*) depict stories that apply to my life.
You can substitute the story with another or change the existing one to say,
"A friend (or colleague) of mine" instead.*

*One summer, as I was preparing to go away on vacation to Greece, a good friend of mine said to me, "I am jealous of you, but it's a white jealousy." I was confused by that, because I had never heard of the term "white jealousy." She told me that in the Russian language, white jealousy was when you feel an innocent twinge of wanting what someone else has. There is no evil in it. After thinking about it for a while, I realized that envy does not always have to be a bad thing. Occasionally, it can be something that pushes you in a good way.

If a friend of yours performed well academically and received an award for their excellence, you may think to yourself, "I wish I could get an award, too." This may push you to work and study harder in school to achieve that goal. This is one way to use an envious thought in a healthy manner. If you wanted to buy a pair of sneakers that you saw someone wearing, instead of wallowing in feelings of self-pity or jealousy, you might decide to save your allowance or your birthday money to get them. It may not happen immediately, but it's a goal you could achieve over time.

*There are times when you may be envious of something you can never have. As an adult, I have reached my maximum height. I know I will never be six feet tall, so there is no point in spending time being envious of tall people. If you have brown eyes, they will never naturally turn blue. Sometimes we need to stop focusing on the things we cannot change and appreciate what we have, instead. My legs did not grow long enough to make me six feet tall, but they are strong and help me walk. My eyes may not be blue, but I can see. Rather than giving our attention to envious thoughts that can only make us feel bad, it is healthier to let them go and focus on your positive qualities. Just as we have to practice acceptance when we face disappointments, we must do the same with certain envious thoughts. If we cannot change the conditions, we have to let the thoughts go.

*One of my cousins has the cutest little toes. I have always thought they make her feet look so pretty. My toes have always been much longer, and in my opinion, not nearly as nice. As much as I wish I could have cute little toes, it is not going to happen, and there is nothing I can do about it. I had to let go of that envious thought, because it didn't benefit me in any way. I decided to be thankful that I had toes to support my body weight and help me stand.

Sometimes people feel envious of others but do not handle it in a healthy or constructive way. For example, if two people are competing to get the last spot on a team, the competitors have a choice to make once the winner is chosen. The gracious way to handle a situation like this, for both the winner and the loser, is to congratulate the competitor on a job well done. Unfortunately, that does not always happen. Sometimes, those who lose the contest behave sorely; they may even accuse the winner of cheating, though the contest was won fairly. There are also people who are poor winners and ridicule the person who lost the contest, thus making the losing person feel even worse. This is not an example of envy, but it sure shows poor sportsmanship.

When an envious thought comes into your mind, you need to ask yourself the question, "Can I use this envious thought in a productive way, or should I lose it?" If the thought is going to inspire you to be better in some way, then keep it, and use it to motivate you toward your goal. But if the thought is going to make you feel bad about yourself or lead you to feel some resentment toward somebody else, then you should lose it. You will be happier and healthier if you choose to let go of envious thoughts that serve no benefit to you.

Activity

In this activity, the children will discuss whether various envious thoughts could be used for good or if they should just "lose" them.

Materials: Prepare a chart like the one shown in chart 7 using a large sheet of chart paper, poster board, or a photocopy. Please feel free to substitute any of the examples with some of your own.

Directions: Read each envious thought out loud. Discuss whether the thought could be used to benefit someone or whether the thought should be "lost."

Chart 7. Use It or Lose It

USE IT	LOSE IT

We're going to play a little game called *Use It or Lose It*. We will review a few envious thoughts that might pop into somebody's mind, and decide if they could use the thought for good or if they should just lose it. If you believe that an envious thought can be helpful in some way, explain how you came to that decision.

- My brother is such a great speller. I wish I could spell as well.
- I love her big, green eyes. I wish I could have eyes like that.
- Your burgers are delicious. I wish I could make burgers like that.
- My ears are too big. I wish mine could look like my friend's.
- That's such a nice purse. I wish I had a purse like that.
- My friend's older sister is so awesome. I wish she could be my sister.

Sometimes I hear a response that surprises me. I would never have imagined a person using a particular envious thought in a positive way. As long as your idea doesn't cause anybody pain and can bring a positive result for you, that's all that matters. And remember, when an envious thought pops into your mind that can't be used for anything positive, let it go. If you can't use it, then lose it, and remind yourself of all the blessings in your life instead.

17
Does That Label Define Me?

Is It the Truth or Just a Stereotype?

(Follow-up lesson to "Tuning In to Your Truth")

If you were hungry and I showed you a silver can of unlabeled food and asked, "Do you want to eat what's inside?" how would you respond? Some people might be bold and say, "Yes, I'm so hungry, I'll give it a chance," not knowing what the can's contents are. Others might say, "Definitely not! What if there is dog food inside? I'm not eating that!" In a case like this, labels on the outside of the can come in very handy. They let us know the exact contents of the item, which allows us to make an informed decision about whether or not we want to buy something—or in this case, eat it.

Aside from food products, we also see labels on items such as clothes, shoes, purses, soaps, detergents, and medicines. Generally, these labels prove to be helpful. For example, if we are allergic to a specific type of food, medicine, or fabric, reading a label can prevent us from eating or using something that could make us ill. Labels can also help us figure out where a product or a person originates from. For example, "This juice is made from California oranges," or

"This cheese is made in France." If you live in Florida, you might refer to yourself as a "Floridian," or "This Italian passport tells me you're from Italy."

Most of us identify with many different labels. Aside from one's name, a person might identify themselves with a relationship label, such as brother, sister, mother, father, grandparent, aunt, or uncle. People also wear professional labels, such as teacher, plumber, doctor, and accountant. We also may label ourselves according to our gender, ethnicity, race, and religion.

The paragraphs with the asterisks (*) apply to my life.
Customize them to describe the labels that personally apply to you.

*There are many labels that I wear. I am proud to call myself a daughter, a sister, a friend, a teacher, a godmother, a member of the Sideratos family, a Christian, a Brooklyn College alumnus, a New Yorker, and an American with Greek family roots.

Sometimes people make inaccurate assumptions about others based on the labels they wear, especially if they are different from their own. Many times, their expectations are based on their experiences with other people who wear one of those same labels.

Here's a simple example. If you grew up in a family with a younger sister who always tattled on you, you may believe that all younger sisters do that, based on your experience. Lots of people have younger sisters, and although some of them might be considered tattle tales, not all of them are. We need to stay mindful to not overgeneralize based on our experiences.

If you are visiting a busy city and encounter one or two rude people on the street, based on your experience, you might assume that all the people in that city are rude, when in fact that may not be the case. You haven't met every person in the city, so it would be unfair to make that judgment. But far too many times, people make the mistake of overgeneralizing and making judgments on an entire group, based on their experience with a few.

*Here's another example to further elaborate. I have an older brother who really excelled in school. In fact, he was the strongest student in his class. A few years later, when I first started school, the principal and teachers recognized my last name and realized I was his younger sister. They initially had the expectation that I might be as strong a student as my brother, which, unfortunately, I wasn't. Their original expectations of me were based *solely* on my last name. Luckily, my parents and teachers realized that though I was a good student, I wasn't going to be the best student in the class and didn't put unnecessary pressure on me to perform as well as my brother. I could only be my best, and that was good enough for them.

Sometimes people start to attach other characterizations to a label, based on past experiences with others. Those identifying traits or characterizations don't necessarily apply to everyone in that category. This overgeneralization is problematic because it may be inaccurate and is far too restricting to describe the whole of a group. These ideas become stereotypes. *A stereotype is an unfair or false belief held by many people about a particular group.* Everybody is different; nobody fits neatly into one box, category, or another person's set of expectations or experiences. People are not that simple, and it's unfair to group them all together as if they are.

*I went to an excellent high school, but for some reason, the students of the school had a reputation for being very snobbish. In fact, I was reluctant to attend the school because I had heard all these rumors about the conceited, stuck-up students. I worried that I would never make friends with anyone there. But lo and behold, the rumors weren't true, and most of the students were delightful. I almost missed the opportunity to attend a great school and make wonderful friendships based on a stereotype of the whole student body. While there were a few students who were snobby, they didn't speak for the whole; in fact, that label didn't fit most of the students.

Activity

In this activity, the children will learn to distinguish between true statements and stereotypes.

Materials: Create a chart like the one shown in chart 8 using chart paper, a poster board, or a dry-erase board.

Directions: Have the children read the pairs of sentences and decide which one in each pair sounds like a stereotype and which one sounds like a truthful sentence. Write each statement in the appropriate column.

Chart 8. Truth vs. Stereotype

A TRUTH	A STEREOTYPE

We're going to play a little game now. I'm going to read several pairs of sentences, and you are going to decide which one sounds truthful and which one sounds like a stereotype. Then we'll write each sentence in the correct column.

Sample Sentence Pairs

I am an athlete who plays on the school's basketball team.
Most athletes are not very smart.

People who live in Texas are Texans.
All Texans are cowboys.

People who have a lot of money are called wealthy.
All wealthy children are spoiled.

The school bus is filled with students who go to school.
All the students on the bus are noisy and disruptive.

My grandparents are older people.
All older people are forgetful and can't hear well.

Baseball is a popular American sport.
All Americans love to watch baseball.

Remember, when you evaluate or judge someone strictly by a label, you will never get a complete picture of who they really are. The only way to truly know someone is by having a personal experience with them. After all, you wouldn't want to be judged solely by the labels you wear.

Should somebody make an incorrect judgment about you based on a stereotype, forgive them for their mistake, but most importantly, don't allow that label to define you. Just be yourself, and show them a new example of what that label could mean. Perhaps you will be the person who redefines their narrow viewpoint and breaks the stereotype.

18
The Kindness Boomerang

(Follow-up lesson to "Penny's Surprise")

Do you know what a boomerang is? It's a curved, flat tool that sometimes look like a capital L. It's usually made of wood, but some are now made of plastic. This tool was historically used to hunt but is now used for sport and competitions. Most of the time when people refer to boomerangs, they are referring to returning boomerangs. The cool thing about this boomerang is that it returns to the person who throws it. Once it's thrown, it arcs through the air in a U shape as it spins, eventually coming back to its thrower. Figure 4 shows what a boomerang looks like.

Figure 4. A Boomerang

Today I want to talk to you about the "Kindness Boomerang." You may be wondering if it is a real thing. Well, it's not something you can go out and buy, but it is a principle that does exist, and I've witnessed it firsthand. I'll explain how the boomerang part works in a moment, but first let me explain the kindness portion of it.

To begin, a person must first decide to perform an act of kindness for another or for a few different people. This kind act does not have to be planned ahead of time, nor does it have to be a grand act; it should just be thoughtful. Here's a simple example: As you walk into a store, you decide to hold the door open for the person behind you. That is a simple act of kindness. Lending a pencil to a friend, helping a family member clean up, cheering up a sad friend, helping someone with their homework. and complimenting a person about something they did well are all examples of kind acts one can perform.

Once a person begins doing kind acts for others, they quickly realize that not only do the recipients of the kind acts feel great, but the doer, too, begins feeling wonderful. Doing kind acts can be so rewarding that it usually inspires people to continue performing more kind acts; the positive effects are almost addictive.

You're probably wondering if this is the boomerang effect I was referring to earlier. Well, it's part of it. While doing nice things for others does make a person feel wonderful, there's more to it than that. What people notice is that the giver of the kind acts suddenly becomes the recipient of kind acts, as well. Kindness will boomerang back to them.

It may not come back to them from the same people, but in fact, sometimes wonderful things will begin to happen to them in unexpected ways, through people they may not even know. The joy and fulfilling effects for everyone involved will be undeniable.

Here's a way that you can test out the boomerang effect for yourself. For the next seven days, practice acts of kindness; do as many wonderful things as possible for others. You can write them down if you wish, or just mentally keep track of how many you do. Then, every day, write down all the wonderful things that begin to happen to you, whether they are big or small. Did somebody hold the door for you? Did somebody compliment you? Has somebody done or made something special for you? These kind acts might begin to show up in a few days, or right away. Most of the time, people realize that they receive even more kindness than they offer.

Now, this doesn't mean that we should do kind things for others only so nice things will happen to us. We should show kindness to others because it's the right thing to do, and because it will fill up our hearts with joy. I'm just challenging you to test the Kindness Boomerang for yourself. Once you experience it, you'll want to continue, and you may even want to ask your friends and family to join in on the fun. Imagine how much more joy would be spread in this world if others got involved. In the end, it will just help make the world a much happier and more wonderful place to live.

Remind the children to keep a record of the kindness they receive after a week's time. Have them report on their findings after the week. Ask them to describe how performing kind acts made them feel, and if there was a particular act that made them feel the most proud. Then ask them to share a few of the kind acts that boomeranged back to them, and whether they would consider doing this activity again, and why.

19
Planning a Trip to a Senior Home

(Follow-up lesson to "A Trip to the Senior Home")

The following is not a lesson to be read to children, but rather,
a guide of how to plan a trip to a senior home.

A trip to a local senior home can be a wonderful experience, whether you decide to go with your class, a youth group, a group of friends, or as an individual. Call the senior home in advance to find out what dates and times work best for a visit. Many seniors welcome the opportunity to spend time with children and adults, as they don't get as many visitors as they would like.

I have personally taken many of my classes, ranging from age six (first graders) to thirteen (seventh graders), to visit senior homes; it always proved to be a very rewarding experience for all of them. Prior to taking children to a senior home, it is beneficial to give them a little background information on what they can expect or encounter once there. They may meet seniors who are not coherent and some who have certain disabilities.

Many children have had experiences with the elderly, but for those who haven't been as exposed, consider preparing them by reading a few stories that feature a senior as one of the main characters. It's important for them to realize that seniors have a great deal of wisdom and knowledge to share based on their life experiences. It is equally as important to expose the children to stories highlighting some of the challenges that come with aging. Among my favorite books I have used before taking my students to the senior home are *The Sunsets of Miss Olivia Wiggins* by Lester L. Laminack, *Nana Upstairs, Nana Downstairs* by Tomie dePaola, and *Wilfrid Gordon McDonald Partridge* by Mem Fox.

Once you arrive at the senior home and introductions have been made, it would be nice for the kids to share a memory or two of theirs with the seniors. They could tell the seniors about a special moment in their life, like a birthday or a wonderful trip they took. They can then ask the seniors to share a story about themselves or their family.

In my experience, younger kids like to have their stories written beforehand in case they get nervous after they arrive. They can also carry a picture of that special moment to help them recall what they want to talk about. On many of the trips I have made to senior homes, I was fortunate enough to be accompanied by my colleague and friend, Calli, and her class. She taught a slightly older class, so we decided to team up a few older students with younger ones. This helped the little ones to feel more comfortable, especially when we first arrived. If this option is not available, grouping children with parents or other adults works just as well.

During our trips to senior homes, the students would sing a few songs for the residents, which we had practiced ahead of time in class. We adults sang along with the music to help give the kids a little more confidence. We also chose well-known sing-along songs that we thought the seniors would be familiar with, hoping to inspire them to sing along, and they usually did. Hearing the children sing brought such joy to so many. During one particular visit, a senior who had not spoken for three months actually began to sing along with the children.

Another idea to consider is to ask a representative of the senior home beforehand if the children would be permitted to play a musical instrument for the seniors (assuming the instrument is not too large to transport). Some homes have small auditorium-like rooms that include a piano, so any child with that ability might be permitted to play for them.

My students and I would also bring the seniors small, inexpensive, handmade gifts, such as a picture frame, a door hanger, or a jewelry box, made of materials like popsicle sticks and foam. The materials were either purchased from a craft store or made from easy-to-assemble kits sold online. Although these gifts were not elaborate or expensive, the seniors really appreciated them. If cost is an issue, children can also draw them a picture or make them a greeting card out of construction paper. Many seniors were very touched by these personal items.

On one occasion, my fifth-grade students and I went to a neighborhood senior center instead of a home, and the center happened to be hosting a holiday party. This, too, was a wonderful experience for my students, as they also had the opportunity to enjoy the party and dance with many of the seniors.

If visiting a senior home is not an option because, for example, there aren't any nearby, an alternative is to have the children visit with an elderly neighbor or relative. The learning that can happen, for both the children and the seniors, is incalculable, especially when they can compare how the lives of children have changed over time, and the reasons behind why this is so. It opens the door to discussions on historical events, family histories, and even the motivations behind certain decisions that family members have made in the past.

As mentioned earlier, I was very blessed to make several visits to one particular senior home with Calli. We would work together throughout the year on a unit of lessons to prepare the children for this experience. We thoroughly enjoyed collaborating on this project, but not nearly as much as our students did. The feedback we received from the children, the seniors, and the parents who chaperoned was absolutely incredible. They were without a doubt some of the most rewarding moments I had experienced as a teacher and a human being. If you have the opportunity to participate in such an experience, especially with children, I highly recommend it.

20
Staying Cheerful During the Waiting Game

(Follow-up lesson to "A Double Test of Patience")

We live in a world where we enjoy getting instant results. People rarely enjoy spending time waiting, but there are times when we all need to be patient and wait for things. What are some things that you have had to wait for?

Sometimes we need to wait only a little while for something we want. For example, if I want to drink a hot cocoa, I might need to wait just a few minutes for it to cool off so I won't burn myself. The same thing happens when we bake cookies. If you try to take them off the cookie sheet without letting them cool first, they fall apart.

There are times when we must wait for a longer period. We wait in line at store registers or to board a bus in order to avoid chaos and be fair to others. We might be in a car stuck in traffic for a half hour or an hour, or traveling in a plane for a few hours to reach our destination. Sometimes we have to wait weeks, months, or years for certain things to happen, such as having seeds grow into a full plant and waiting for a baby to walk. That's because there is a natural timing to some things. It takes time for a plant to sprout and develop its roots to grow. The same applies to babies. Their muscles require time to strengthen enough for them to take their first steps.

Many times, though, we can become cranky and impatient when we need to wait for things. We prefer things to be done instantly or handled in a timelier way. I know I have become impatient when a waiter or waitress was taking too long to take my order, especially when I was very hungry. Perhaps you have lost your patience with a younger sibling or friend because they still haven't learned to tie their shoelaces, even though you've shown them how to do it at least twenty times. Have you ever felt like your patience was being tested waiting for something? How did you handle it? Looking back on it now, do you think you could have handled it better? If so, how?

Being patient for things can be challenging, and the irony is, the only way to develop patience is by waiting. Think of it as a muscle that needs to be developed; it doesn't happen overnight - it takes time and effort. I came to the realization that if I'm going to spend time waiting, instead of being grouchy about it, I would try to enjoy myself during the "waiting game." Oddly enough, sometimes I get so involved in these activities during my wait that it seems the time just flies by. Instead of spending my time complaining and being miserable, which ultimately never changes the wait time anyway, I actually enjoy myself, instead.

Activity

This activity will inspire the children to come up with activities to do when they have waiting periods.

Materials: To prepare, make note of the sample ideas for activities in chart 9. (You do not need to record these suggestions on the chart if the children don't like them.) Then create a chart like the one shown in chart 10 using chart paper, a poster board, or a dry-erase board.

Directions: Ask the children to share some ideas about what they would enjoy doing during a brief waiting period, and then during a longer waiting period. Record them in the appropriate column in the chart.

Chart 9. Sample Activities for the Waiting Game

DURING A BRIEF WAITING PERIOD	DURING A LONGER WAITING PERIOD
Practice deep breathing.	Help somebody else.
Listen to music or sing along.	Work on a project.
Read a chapter in a book.	Watch a DVD.
Talk to someone waiting on the line with you.	Call a friend.
Think about someone or something that makes you happy	

Chart 10. Activities to Stay Cheerful during the Waiting Game

DURING A BRIEF WAITING PERIOD	DURING A LONGER WAITING PERIOD

Let's do a little activity now where we can share some ideas about what we could do to make the "waiting game" a little more enjoyable. On one side of the chart, we're going to write our ideas about what we could do during a brief waiting period, and on the other side, we'll record our ideas about what we could do during a longer waiting period.

Teachers, after you model this activity with the class, it would be helpful for each child to create their own personal chart to refer to in the future.

Remember, people like different things, so what is enjoyable to you may not be enjoyable to somebody else. Some people like to sing or hum, others prefer to read. One person enjoys doing puzzles, another enjoys listening to music. If you encounter an idea that you wouldn't enjoy doing, don't be critical of it, just come up with more ideas of your own.

The next time you need to practice a little patience, try choosing something to do from your list. If you need to wait anyway, you may as well try to make it a more enjoyable experience.

21
The Love Week Project

(Follow-up lesson to "Love Is a Way to Live")

Today I am going to invite you to take part in the *Love Week Project*. You may be wondering if this has something to do with Valentine's Day, but it doesn't. Although you may decide to use the week of Valentine's Day as a great time of year to begin this project, it can be done on any or all of the fifty-two weeks of the year.

Activity

In this activity, the children will share their definitions of what the word "love" means to them.

Materials: For this activity you will need a very large sheet of chart paper or poster board and a marker or pen.

Directions: Draw the outline of a heart as big as possible on the paper, as seen in figure 5. Write the word "love" in the middle of it. Ask the children to tell you their definitions of love, and write them inside the heart shape.

To begin this project, we must have a clear definition of what the word *love* means. What does the word *love* mean to you? We're going to write your definitions inside this outline of a heart.

Figure 5. Heart

As you listen to each child's response, ask them to explain their basis for their definition. "What made you think of that definition? Could you give me an example of your definition?"

After you have recorded the responses, if it has not already come up in your discussion, make sure to explain that "love" is a verb (an action word) because it requires some work. Most people think of it as a feeling, but it is much more than that. One of my favorite definitions of the word is a quote by Joyce Meyer. She says, "Love is not a mere feeling, it's a decision about how we will behave and treat people." You may use this definition or a variation of it.

We show love to others through our actions and behavior. Telling someone you care about them is wonderful, but demonstrating that love with actions usually touches their heart in a special way and shows them you really mean it. We can show people our love by doing nice things for them or by being considerate of their feelings. For example, if a friend is sick, giving them a call to find out how they are doing is an easy way to show your love. Helping a loved one carry heavy bags of groceries so they don't have to struggle is another way to demonstrate your love.

Activity

In this activity, you will introduce the children to the Love Week Project. You do not need to do any preparation for this project other than to read the detailed description of the project, below.

The children will spend a week participating in the project. At the end of the week, the children will share their experiences and describe how the experience affected them and their loved ones. Ask them if their experience changed the way they would define "love" now, and whether they wish to add any new definitions to the outlined heart.

Are you ready to take part in the Love Week Project? The idea behind the Love Week Project is to choose one week during which you will show your love even more than usual to the people you care about. Each day, you will choose one person to be the recipient of your special love, attention, and appreciation. You may choose to do one very nice thing or several small things for them.

It is not necessary to buy them expensive gifts; just show them your love in thoughtful ways. Perhaps you can make them a card, draw a picture, or write a poem or letter telling them how special they are to you. You may decide to make something for them, like a sandwich, a special dessert, or a homemade craft item. If you are musical, you might want to play or sing a special song for them, or if you like to dance, perhaps you could perform a special dance.

Another option is to be that person's special helper for a day. Instead of doing one thing, do a few minor favors for them throughout the day, such as walking the dog, putting the groceries away, playing a game with them, reading them a story, or making their bed. You choose how you will show your love to them.

I am certain that you can come up with better ideas than I can. Before you begin the day, spend a few moments thinking about that person and what they might enjoy. I can guarantee that no matter what you choose to do for them, it will fill their heart with much joy and love.

You may decide that you want to show your love to one very special person for more than one day. That's fine, but try to include as many different loved ones as you can in the Love Week Project. If there are more than seven people you want to show your love to, continue for as many days as you like. As I mentioned earlier, you can take part in the Love Week Project for as many weeks as you like.

After taking part in the Love Week Project, I'd like to us to come back and share about our experiences.

22
There's Always Room for More Love

Our Ever-Expanding Hearts

(Follow-up lesson to "There's Always Room for More")

The paragraphs with the asterisks (*) tell stories that apply to either me or my family but may not apply to yours. You can change the story to refer to a friend or family that you know instead.

*When my family and I go shopping, we like to buy in bulk. If hairspray or shampoo are on sale, we'll buy a large quantity of them, and then attempt to squeeze the extra bottles into our cabinets along with all the other items packed in there. The same thing happens with our groceries. We'll buy big packages of things from a wholesale club store, after which I'm left struggling to find room for everything to fit. Sometimes, as I'm trying to squeeze things onto an overcrowded shelf, I end up knocking something else down on the other side.

There are times when I wish I could make my shelves and cabinets stretch to fit everything I want to put in there, but they have a finite amount of space, and can't grow and expand.

Unlike the shelves and cabinets, some things have the potential to grow and expand and fit multitudes of things. We can expand our minds by studying and gaining more knowledge. That doesn't mean that our brain is literally getting larger in size every time we learn something, but over time, more information, experiences, and memories get stored in there, much like a powerful computer whose database is growing.

The heart is an important organ that not only pumps our blood and helps spread oxygen to all the parts of our body, but also is the symbolic place where people say our love is stored. Like our minds, our hearts have the capacity to expand and hold an infinite amount of love in them. The longer we are alive, the more opportunities we have to fill our hearts with love. Believe it or not, sometimes people forget just how much our hearts can stretch and how much love they can fit inside of them. This may occur when somebody they love brings a new person into their life. They fear that the new person in the circle might take away some of their love. Here are a few examples to help clarify what I mean.

There are times when a family welcomes a new baby into their home. This is a very exciting time for most families but can also be a little stressful, as a new baby initially requires a lot of extra time and attention. Babies need to be fed and changed very often and keep their parents awake throughout most of the night.

During this early stage, if there is another child or other children in the family, they may not enjoy as much of their parents' time and attention as they used to. What the children need to realize is that their parents still love them just as much as they did before. While this baby may require a little extra care at first, their parents had to do the same for them when they were babies. The baby did not replace the space in their parents' heart, it just stretched it. Did you ever feel this way? How did you handle the situation? What helped you feel better?

*I felt like this once when I was in grade school. My best friend, Helen, befriended a new girl in our class, and when they started spending time together, I became jealous and thought Helen wouldn't feel the same way about me any more. Although Helen never stopped being my friend and told me repeatedly that she wanted us all to be friends, I had a tough time believing her. In my mind,

I was afraid that if the other girl became one of Helen's best friends, I would no longer be as special to her. I didn't know that both her heart and mine had the ability to expand.

Like the cans of food on the shelf, I thought that if she made room for her new friend, I might fall off the other side. It took a little while, but Helen did finally convince me that I wasn't getting pushed out of her heart just because somebody else entered it. Eventually, all three of us became friends. Has that or something similar ever happened to you? Will you share your story with me?

Here's another example where a person might need to allow their heart to stretch. Sometimes, a new person becomes part of our family through marriage. A parent sometimes remarries after a divorce or after their spouse passes away. This might particularly upset the children or make them feel nervous, especially if they don't know their new stepparent very well.

Some children feel uncomfortable because, in their mind, they feel like their other parent is being replaced by somebody new. They might even feel guilty about loving that new person. However, there is no reason to feel that way. *No person is replaceable, and neither is the love you feel for them.* Rather, the children should see it as an opportunity to allow their heart to grow and stretch.

On occasion, new marriages also bring stepbrothers, stepsisters, and even new step-grandparents into a family. This doesn't mean that any of your other family members will get booted out. The heart has room for an infinite amount of love. The love we have to give is not a limited amount that needs to be shared; no one will get a smaller percentage of your love when you begin caring for more people. In fact, life is richer and more beautiful when we stretch our heart and let it overflow with love.

*(For this next part, you will need to use a balloon as a visual aid.
Use the largest balloon you can find.)*

Think of your heart as the biggest balloon in the world. When we look at this deflated balloon, it doesn't look like it can hold very much inside. As I start to fill it up with air, it expands more and more, and can double, triple, or quadruple in size. This is similar to the way our hearts work.

(Inflate the balloon to show its expansion possibilities.)

The biggest difference between this balloon and your heart is that the heart can stretch immeasurably and will never pop from being overfilled. There's always room for more love. My wish for you is that by the time you get to be old and gray, your heart becomes so stretched and filled with love that it completely overflows, bringing you and the people you encounter more joy than you could ever imagine.

www.ingramcontent.com/pod-product-compliance
Lightning Source LLC
Chambersburg PA
CBHW051353070526
44584CB00025B/3745